Reinventing
IKEA

Disclaimer: Working with sharp tools, using a step ladder, and working with electrical wiring all are poten-
tially hazardous. Always use appropriate safety equipment, such as eye protection, when using power tools,
and don't perform any tasks you don't feel qualified to carry out. The steps we've suggested on each of the
projects are suggestions, not hard and fast rules. When in doubt, ask for help from a qualified electrician,
carpenter, or other professional.

A Note on Measurements: Because IKEA products are originally sized in metric units, measurements in this
book are given in USC and metric units. Readers who wish to tackle one of the building projects in this book
are encouraged to review the whole project carefully in relation to the IKEA product being modified, and then
adjust lumber needs to suit the method of construction they decide to follow.

Neither the IKEA Group nor any of its companies has any association with the publisher or contents of this
book. The text is solely the responsibility of the publisher, and the IKEA Group is in no way liable for it.

For Höebeke:
Graphic Designer: Audrey Hette
Photogravure: APS Chromostyle

Library of Congress Control Number: 2016932043

ISBN: 978-1-4197-2267-7

Printed and bound in Italy
10 9 8 7 6 5 4 3 2 1

Abrams books are available at special discounts when purchased in quantity for premiums and promotions as
well as fundraising or educational use. Special editions can also be created to specification. For details, contact
specialsales@abramsbooks.com or the address below.

ABRAMS
The Art of Books

115 West 18th Street
New York, NY 10011
abramsbooks.com

Reinventing

IKEA

By Isabelle Bruno and Christine Baillet

Abrams Image, New York

INTRODUCTION

Kura, Knuff, Godmorgon, Trofast—the chronicle of household décor is being rewritten, and its new language is Swedish. It's so simple for do-it-yourselfers to adapt IKEA's modular furnishings to suit their creative desires.

Actually, we see this DIY craze as a Do As You Are trend: Follow your heart and create your own décor. Give free expression to your personality, expertise, and lifestyle. Put your talents on display, and encourage family members to participate. You'll eventually find yourselves building a DAYA house together. It will be practical, of course, but also a bit crazy, a little crafty, and full of good cheer.

As you explore the world of DAYA, use *Reinventing Ikea* as a guide: Check out the projects for ideas, and give your imagination free rein. This book shows you how to create unique objects from standardized pieces of furniture. Who knows? You might create a masterpiece. Experiment with being an architect, designer, or inventor next weekend—build something new!

We'll provide plenty of helpful tips for creating successful DIY projects. You'll likely encounter some technical issues as you go along, and you'll need to tackle those based on the individual features of your home. Some of these projects require specific skills as well, but many are so simple that your children can enjoy the creative process along with you. Family DAYA projects are fun for all!

Remember, this book is not intended to make you an über DIYer. And we want to emphasize that it's essential to observe the obvious precautions and to always follow the manufacturer's instructions for using their products and tools. Anything involving electricity or plumbing will require expert assistance and strict compliance with safety recommendations. Wall-hung items and tall pieces must be secured according to professional standards.

We've divided the projects into four categories—simple, medium, advanced, and expert—based on their complexity and the time required for their completion. IKEA's star product lines receive some special attention. *Kallax, Frosta,* and *Kura* are ideal for creative experimentation and lend themselves to any project you could possibly dream up. Maybe you'll develop your own projects along the way.

Are you ready to get started? Want to jazz up your décor and have a terrific time while you're at it? Then welcome to the world of DAYA!

level

SIMPLE

DRESS UP YOUR DRESSER WITH STICKERS!

© Inter IKEA Systems B.U.

All parents want to foster independence in their children, especially when getting dressed for the day. But how can you actually help kids accomplish daily tasks on their own? Sometimes all it takes is one simple idea Therese Larsson found a way to boost children's organizational ability and encourage independence, even if they can't yet read: She added stickers to her *Malm* chest that represent the contents of each drawer. After all, a picture is worth a thousand words! Make sure to check the weather report before opening the drawers and fishing around for what to wear—pants or a skirt today?

THE STICKERS MAKE IT EASY FOR CHILDREN TO FIND EVERYTHING THEY'LL NEED FOR THE DAY.

SUPPLIES

From IKEA:
• **Malm 6-drawer chest**

Other:
• **9 sheets heavy paper for patterns**
• **1 roll or 9 sheets black adhesive film**

TOOLS:
• **Pencil**
• **Utility knife**
• **Cutting mat**
• **Roller**

HOW TO DO IT

1. Cut out a pattern for each category of clothing on a sheet of heavy paper.

2. Using a pencil, trace the outlines of each pattern onto the back of the sheet of adhesive film.

3. Cut out each shape using a utility knife.

4. To avoid bubbles, use a roller to stick the pictograms to the drawers.

Design: Therese Larsson

RUSTIC PLACE SETTINGS

IKEA's lifestyle blog *Livet Hemma* is full of suggestions for transforming standard household objects with a few brushstrokes, or even a wood-burning tool. This project encourages you to experiment with pokerwork—which means "writing with fire"—and personalize kitchenware. The more basic the utensil, the better it lends itself to imaginative designs. A great way to start is to decorate a wooden cutting board and *Rört* wooden eating utensils with leaves and flowers. Once you master simple designs, you can move on to more complicated patterns or add personalized messages, making the perfect housewarming gift.

SUPPLIES

From IKEA:
- *Rört* oak forks and spoons
- *Proppmätt* chopping board

TOOLS:
- Very fine sandpaper
- Small vise that can be fastened to a table or workbench
- Pencil or rubber stamp with desired design
- Wood-burning tool
- Wood-burning tips of various widths
- Fireproof surface for safely cooling the tips

HOW TO DO IT

1. Gently sand the surface of each object. Follow the grain of the wood.

2. Wipe the surface thoroughly with a damp rag.

3. Make sure the object is held steady on a stable surface. You may wish to secure the handles of the utensils in a vise.

4. Draw or stamp your design on the wood. If you're not a drawing expert, opt for a simple design and practice first on paper. In our example, a central line with small strokes along the sides produces an attractive foliage pattern. (More experienced artists who can draw directly with the wood-burning tool can skip this step.)

5. Attach the tip to the burner, then heat it up.

6. Trace over your drawing with the point of the hot stylus, using light pressure. (Or draw directly onto the utensil.)

7. Change the tips as needed to create your design. When you've finished, let the tips cool on a fireproof surface before cleaning them according to the manufacturer's instructions.

Photos : © Inter IKEA Systems B.U.

Do small things with great love

BEGINNERS TEND TO PRESS DOWN ON THE WOOD-BURNING TIP TOO HARD, WHICH MAKES THE LINES LESS CLEARLY DEFINED. WE SUGGEST A FEW PRELIMINARY TESTS USING WOOD SCRAPS.

STUFFED ANIMALS TAKE CENTER STAGE!

© Inter IKEA Systems B.V.

> There they all are, those childhood friends—some funny, some scary, all beloved. Even the ones with squashed heads and missing eyes. Let these loyal companions step into the spotlight as lively wall décor. Children can easily reach in to grab their current favorite.

SUPPLIES

From IKEA:
- *Alseda* ottoman

Other:
- Anchors, screws, and hooks suitable for the wall surface

TOOLS:
- Utility knife or scissors
- Drill or screwdriver, as needed to attach hanging hardware

HOW TO DO IT

To convert the ottoman to wall décor, just cut the banana fiber covering off of the metal armature and hang it on the wall. That's it! Please note that the metal frame weighs more than 9 pounds (4 kg), so carefully choose hanging hardware that will securely fasten it to the wall. Use a stud finder to locate the wall framing and screw the metal frame directly to the studs.

DON'T HIDE THOSE STUFFED ANIMALS AWAY IN A CHEST. MAKE A COLORFUL DISPLAY IN YOUR CHILD'S BEDROOM.

Design : Mommo Design

GET A GRIP ON YOUR CUTTING BOARDS

The DIY movement is all about adding a dash of personality to commonplace objects. In the case of cutting boards, this can simply mean wrapping ornamental leather cords around the handles. For this project, the focus is on how you knot the laces and arrange the rivets. Take a look at *Livet Hemma*'s design ideas here, then strike out on your own.

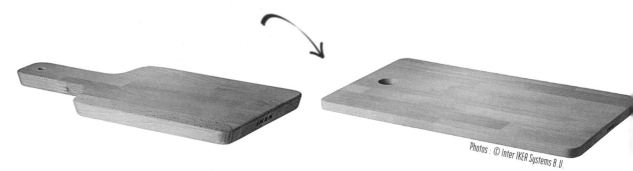

Photos : © Inter IKEA Systems B.U.

HOW TO DO IT

FOR A BOARD WITH A HANDLE:

Use tightly laced fine cords to decorate the handle.

FINE CORDS:

Version 1 (bottom center): Make a "sawtooth" lacing on the handle. In this type of lacing, the visible upper lacing is horizontal, and the lacing beneath is on the diagonal.

Version 2 (upper left): Lay the cord flat and place the handle in the middle, with the two ends of the cord equidistant from it. Lace tightly by wrapping each end of the cord around the handle. When you reach the top, slide the ends of the cord through the hole and knot them together.

SUPPLIES

From IKEA:
• *Proppmätt* chopping board in the desired style (with handle, without handle, with groove)

Other:
• Leather cords and laces of various sizes and colors (12 in./30 cm minimum for simply wrapped handles; 3 ft./1 m or more for models with laced handles)
• Rivets
• Carpet tacks

TOOLS :

• Revolving punch pliers
• Hammer

Design : IKEA Livet Hemma

CARING FOR
YOUR CUTTING BOARDS:
DON'T PUT THEM IN THE
DISHWASHER, AND AVOID
CONTACT WITH WATER.
CONDITION THE LEATHER
EVERY SIX MONTHS.

FOR BOARDS WITH OR WITHOUT HANDLES:

FINE CORDS (LOWER LEFT):

Group three cords and tie a knot at one end. Slide the loose ends through the cutting board's hole and braid about two-thirds of the way down. Tie the braid off with a fourth cord, leaving the loose ends free.

MEDIUM CORDS:

For boards without a hole (upper right): Make a loop with the cord. Attach the loop to the cutting board's surface with a carpet tack.

For boards with a hole (top center): Attach the cord to the board's handle using a carpet tack. Slide the cord through the hole. Secure the end with a rivet.

WIDE CORDS:

Version 1 (center): Slide the cord through the board's hole. Attach the ends together with two rivets.

Version 2 (lower right): Fold your cord in half. Slide the loop through the cutting board's hole. Pull the ends of the cord through the loop, then secure them with a rivet.

A COOL RIDE ON RAILS

© Inter IKEA Systems B.V.

 We all know that kids love toy cars. They're not so fond of tidying up, though, and those booby traps on wheels are a real safety hazard. Abby Lawson discovered a foolproof way to get little ones to exercise control over their runaway playthings: magnets! Miniature cars, trains, and other miniatures will defy the laws of gravity as long as they've got a little ferromagnetic metal in their makeup.

SUPPLIES

From IKEA:
- *Grundtal* stainless-steel magnetic knife racks

Other:
- Screws and anchors

TOOLS:
- Pencil
- Screwdriver
- Drill
- Measuring tape

HOW TO DO IT

1. Decide where you want to mount the racks, making sure the child can easily reach the toys.

2. Mount the racks on the wall, following the installation instructions provided.

3. Check to make sure the rack is securely attached.

4. Attach toy cars to the rack for easy access.

THESE MAGNETIC RACKS
NOW HAVE USE
OUTSIDE OF THE KITCHEN.
FORGET STAINLESS
STEEL KNIVES—STORE
FLASHY TOY CARS IN A
COLORFUL DISPLAY.

Design : Abby Lawson

THE MONDRIAN DESK

© Inter IKEA Systems B.U.

Piet Mondrian's unique abstract compositions were first introduced to the world in the early 1920s and evolved over the following decades. Their brilliant primary colors of blue, yellow, and red separated by rectilinear black bars inspired De Stijl artists of this period, and Mondrian's paintings have continued to influence generations. From the dresses in Yves Saint Laurent's 1965 collection to contemporary furniture, fabrics, and wallpapers, Mondrian's "pure reality" enhances any available surface, even your workspace.

SUPPLIES

From IKEA:
- *Micke* computer workstation

Other:
- Matte or high-gloss acrylic paint (black, red, yellow, blue)
- Painter's masking tape

TOOLS:
- Very fine sandpaper
- Brush or small roller

HOW TO DO IT

1. Before assembling the desk and its wall unit: Lightly sand the surfaces to be painted and wipe them thoroughly.

2. Protect the horizontal surfaces with painter's masking tape.

3. Paint the trim black (one or two layers, depending on the quality of your paint).

4. Let the surfaces dry completely (48 hours minimum), then protect the trim with painter's masking tape.

5. Apply the first coat of paint. After it has dried thoroughly (check the paint manufacturer's recommendations), sand lightly and apply a second coat if necessary. Continue until you have painted the primary colors in the desired areas. Allow all surfaces to dry.

6. Assemble the desk, following the instructions provided.

FUN ON WHEELS

© Inter IKEA Systems B.V.

❝❞ Furniture and product designer Sam Johnson has given a lot of thought to toy design. Looking for something whimsical for his toddlers that could be cobbled together from almost nothing, he found the perfect solution. Kids will entertain themselves for hours zipping around on this sturdy little steed, with its strong back and pivoting wheels. A butcher block base and storage bin seat are the two basic components. This might seem a little too minimal without Sam's canny additions: handles in the form of two cabinet-knob ears or an alien's antennae, and stick-on eyes to brighten up the face.

HOW TO DO IT

1. Drill two holes through the board, one at the front center and one at the back, so you can insert the cable ties. Make holes in the corresponding locations on the top edge of the bin.

2. Drill two holes in the bottom of the bin. Attach the knob ears by screwing them into the holes or the rope handle by feeding each end into the holes and knotting them. Hot glue a plastic stick or chopstick to the backside of the bin for a tail.

3. Attach a caster to each corner on the bottom of the board. Secure the bin tightly to the board with ties.

SUPPLIES

From IKEA:
- *Aptitlig* butcher block board (or another board of your choice)
- *Trofast* storage bin (16½ x 11¾ x 4 in./42 x 30 x 10 cm)
- 2 cabinet knobs, such as *Värde* (or a length of rope)
- *Algot* casters (or other casters)

Other:
- 2 heavy-duty cable ties
- 1 flexible plastic rod (carried by shops that sell supplies for scale models) or 1 chopstick
- 16 screws for the wheels
- Round self-adhesive felt floor protector pads or stick-on googly eyes

TOOLS:
- Drill
- Glue gun
- Screwdriver

SAM NAMED HIS TOY SKAPA—THE WORD MEANS "CREATE" IN SWEDISH.

Design : Sam Johnson

PAINT THIS CHAIR!

© Inter IKEA Systems B.U.

A word of advice to all you life-coach pros: Peruse DIY blogs. They're brimming with great suggestions to help people keep cool, manage stress, and build self-confidence. This is important to keep in mind, because you'll need all that (along with a little chutzpah) to take a high-backed chair upholstered in white and lavish it with freehand graphic décor. But don't be intimidated! This project does call for concentration and effort, but all you actually need is a permanent marker. This bold homemade pattern was created by textile designer Caitlin Wilson.

A RANDOM SCATTERING OF POLKA DOTS CREATES A SENSATIONAL EFFECT!

SUPPLIES

From IKEA:
• **Harry** chairs

Other:
• **Permanent marker or fabric marker (3 mm)**

HOW TO DO IT

1. If you like, start with a trial run: Pin a fabric scrap to a vertical support (you could use the back of the chair, protected with a waterproof cover, for example), uncap the marker, and give it a shot. A random look is the charm of this design.

You're not aiming for perfection. Just let yourself go!

2. When you're ready, decorate the chair itself. Choose whatever color and pattern you like!

TO DO :

buy juice
pick up cards
dry cleaning

HOMAGE TO DICK BRUNA

© Inter IKEA Systems B.V.

" Created by Dutch artist Dick Bruna in 1955, Miffy recently celebrated a landmark birthday. Bruna dreamed up this little rabbit to entertain his daughter. The original Miffy was a simple stuffed toy with floppy ears. Later on, she got a bit chubbier, pricked up those ears, and began standing on her own two feet and sporting a jaunty skirt. Miffy became a beloved icon for baby boomers and their own offspring. Books, TV series, stamps, and knickknacks proliferated. Embodying the gentle world of childhood, Miffy has become a cherished character across the world—and with this lamp, she will light up your bedtime routine. No one can be indifferent to her charms.

SUPPLIES

From IKEA:
• *Fado* table lamp

Other:
• Permanent marker
• White card stock
• Epoxy, polyurethane, or UV glue stick for a glue gun, or double-sided tape
• LED lightbulb (emits less heat)

TOOLS:
• Scissors
• Glue gun, if needed

HOW TO DO IT

1. Using the marker, draw the rabbit's eyes and mouth on the surface of the lamp.

2. Draw the ears on a sheet of card stock, adding about 1 in. (2.5 cm) at the bottom of each ear to serve as a base.

3. Cut out the ears, fold the bases toward the back to form flaps, and attach the flaps to the lamp using glue or tape.

4. If you used glue, wait until it dries completely (see manufacturer's recommendations) before switching on the lamp. Use an LED, to avoid creating too much heat.

Do not leave the lamp on while unattended.

Design : Mommo Design

© mommodesign.com

MARTIN KRUSCHE'S
MR. MOON

© Inter IKEA Systems B.V.

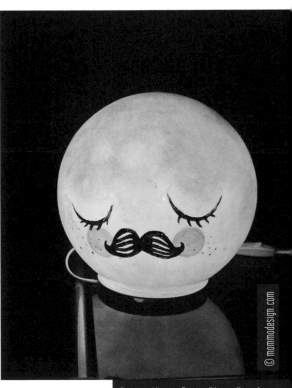

Design : Mommo Design/Martin Krusche

" We'll never know how many planets there are in artist Martin Krusche's unique universe inhabited by human-headed animals, dreamlike scenes, and otherworldly objects. One thing's for sure—it includes a moon. A mustachioed, debonair moon, whose gentle glow washes over everything as he slumbers serenely on.

SUPPLIES

From IKEA:
• *Fado* table lamp

Other:
• **Black permanent marker**
• **Pink permanent marker**

HOW TO DO IT

1. Draw Mr. Moon's face freehand. Practice first if you like by taping a sheet of paper over the globe.

2. Rub the black marker onto a rag and pat the lamp's surface to create the effect of clouds.

Do not leave the lamp on while unattended.

25

A WALL OF PLATES

❝ What's the best way to liven up a humdrum white wall in a high-ceilinged room? Here's the *Livet Hemma* bloggers' stylish, contemporary take on the traditional decorative plate display. Far from a dated cliché, their arrangement is inspired by the varied shapes and sizes of plates embellished with improvised designs, stamps, and colors. A chic concept for knockout décor.

Photos : © Inter IKEA Systems B.U.

HOW TO DO IT

1. Wipe the plates with white vinegar.

2. Decorate the plates however you like using the markers or paint. Let them dry if necessary.

3. Lay out the plates on the floor to create an attractive arrangement before mounting them on the wall.

MOUNT PLATES TO WALL:

For a free-floating look, you can use heavy-duty Disc Hangers, or you can use wire plate hangers, which come in a variety of sizes.

Note: These plates are intended for decorative purposes only, and should not be used for serving food.

SUPPLIES

From IKEA:
- *Färgrik* and *Värdera* plates (or other plate assortment)

Other:
- White vinegar
- Special paint or markers for unfired porcelain
- Wall-mounting hardware for plates

TOOLS:

- Brushes in various sizes, if needed for paints
- Hammer or screwdriver

LET YOUR
IMAGINATION RUN WILD
AND GIVE THOSE
PLATES A PERSONALITY.

Design : IKEA Livet Hemma

CIRCUS-INSPIRED BED LEGS

"This DIY project is child's play—and it's fun to do with kids. You use stencils and bright, cheerful colors to transform simple bed legs into decorative accessories. *Livet Hemma's* pretty designs were inspired by the graphic patterns of the circus.

ALTERNATIVE:
YOU CAN USE ORDINARY MASKING TAPE TO MARK OFF YOUR DESIGNS INSTEAD OF STENCILS. AND FEEL FREE TO COME UP WITH YOUR OWN DESIGNS FOR THE BED LEGS!

HOW TO DO IT

THE STENCIL:

1. Trace an outline the size of the bed leg onto a piece of cardboard.

2. Place a glass on the lower part of the cardboard shape and trace a circle, or use a compass.

3. Then draw a triangle pointing downward from the top of the shape. Remember, the shapes you draw should not go all the way to the edge of the stencil.

4. Use a utility knife to cut out the stencils from the cardboard following your outlines.

SUPPLIES

From IKEA:
• 4 *Sultan* bed legs in oak

Other:
• Acrylic paint in the colors of your choice

TOOLS:
• Sheet of cardboard
• Scissors or utility knife
• Masking tape
• Fine sandpaper
• Paintbrush

THE BED LEG:

1. Attach the stencil to the front of the leg using masking tape.

2. Lightly sand the uncovered portion of the surface of the leg. Then wipe it off and apply the paint.

3. Repeat on all sides of the leg, allowing adequate time for the paint to dry.

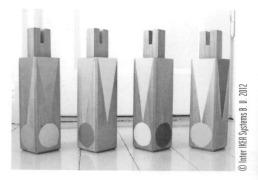

WHY NOT PERSONALIZE YOUR CUPS AND PLATES!

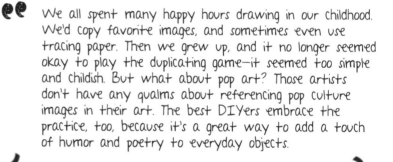

"We all spent many happy hours drawing in our childhood. We'd copy favorite images, and sometimes even use tracing paper. Then we grew up, and it no longer seemed okay to play the duplicating game—it seemed too simple and childish. But what about pop art? Those artists don't have any qualms about referencing pop culture images in their art. The best DIYers embrace the practice, too, because it's a great way to add a touch of humor and poetry to everyday objects.

Photos : © Inter IKEA Systems B.U.

SUPPLIES

From IKEA:

• White plates and cups from the *IKEA 365+* line (or any tableware you prefer)

Other:

• Collected images that appeal to you (or, of course, you can draw freehand)

• Marker for use on porcelain (choose a nontoxic marker if the dishware will come in contact with food)

TOOLS:

• Transfer paper for copying designs onto porcelain

• Pencil

HOW TO DO IT

1. Clean the plate with white vinegar and a paper towel.

2. Decide what images you want for your dishes. Use the carbon paper and a pencil to transfer each image onto the cleaned cup or plate.

3. Use the marker to draw over the traced lines. If necessary, go over the design several times to make sure the ink adheres in a uniform deep-black line. (It's a good idea to rub the marker on paper before you begin to draw on the ceramic surface.)

4. Allow dishware to dry fully before using.

Note: To make the dishware with the designs dishwasher-safe, place dishware in cold oven. Preheat the oven to 350°F, and then bake for 30 minutes. Turn the oven off and allow the dishware to cool completely before removing.

IMAGINATION IS THE ONLY GUIDE YOU'LL NEED FOR THIS DIY PROJECT. JUST FOLLOW YOUR FANCIES.

Design : Nadia Soledad Anton

A DELECTABLY LIGHT TREAT

" Gastronomes aren't the only people inspired by cookware. Kitchen staples often stimulate the creative juices of designers, who playfully repurpose and transform practical objects into decorative whimsies. If cupcakes aren't your cup of tea, *Drömmar* baking cups can be turned into little lampshades. This luminous garland is a treat from Mommo Design that you can enjoy in every room of the house.

© Inter IKEA Systems B. U.

Design : Mommo Design

© mommodesign.com

SUPPLIES

From IKEA:
- *Drömmar* baking cups
- *Särdal* lighting chain

TOOLS:
- **Utility knife**
- **Pencil**

HOW TO DO IT

1. Draw a little X on the bottom of each baking cup and use a utility knife to cut along the lines.

2. Slide the liners over the garland's bulbs.

3. Make sure you follow appropriate safety measures when installing the garland. Do not allow the bulbs to touch the paper baking cups.

Do not leave the lights on while unattended.

FILTERED LIGHT RADIATES THROUGH THE GARLAND'S IMPROVISED SHADES.

HEART NIGHT-LIGHT

© Inter IKEA Systems B.V.

This simple project turns a heart-shaped silicone baking mold into a night-light. The soft, comforting glow that radiates from the blue-tinted nightstand fixture means your baby won't reproach you for having a heart of stone when you turn off the bedroom light.

TRANSFORM A SILICONE HEART INTO A NIGHT-LIGHT TO DISPEL BEDTIME FEARS.

Design: Mommo Design

© mommodesign.com

SUPPLIES

From IKEA:
- *Sockerkaka* baking mold, heart-shaped, light blue
- *Särdal* lighting chain

Other:
- 8 Ping-Pong balls
- Epoxy or polyurethane glue

TOOLS:
- Permanent marker
- Awl

HOW TO DO IT

1. Using the marker, make eight evenly spaced marks around the rim of the mold where the lights will be inserted.

2. Use the awl to make a hole at each mark.

3. Make a hole in each Ping-Pong ball.

4. Slide the bulbs through the holes in the bottom of the mold and then insert them into the balls.

5. Attach the balls to the mold with glue, and allow to dry. Let the remaining lights on the chain hang behind the night-light.

Do not leave the night-light on while unattended.

33

TURN THE TABLE!

© Inter IKEA Systems B.V.

Here's a repurposing idea with a twist, sort of: Regina Morrison transformed a table . . . into *another table!* Maybe the word *swapping* is more appropriate in this case. All you do is remove the original legs, adjust the look of the tabletop, and attach new legs. It's an easy turnaround, and the results are spectacular.

SUPPLIES

From IKEA:
• *Jokkmokk* table (sold with 4 chairs) or *Ingo* table

Other:
• Fine sandpaper
• Medium sandpaper, if needed
• 4 metal hairpin legs with appropriate screws
• Liquid wood stain of your choice (light gray is shown in this example)

TOOLS:
• Screwdriver
• Sander or sanding block
• Paintbrush

HOW TO DO IT

1. Remove the table's legs and fittings, retaining only the top.

2. If the wood is unfinished, sand it lightly. If the wood is finished, sand it until the varnish is removed, starting with medium sandpaper, then finishing with fine.

3. Wipe off the dust and apply the stain, following the directions on the label.

4. Screw on the metal legs about 1 in. (2.5 cm) from the edges of the tabletop.

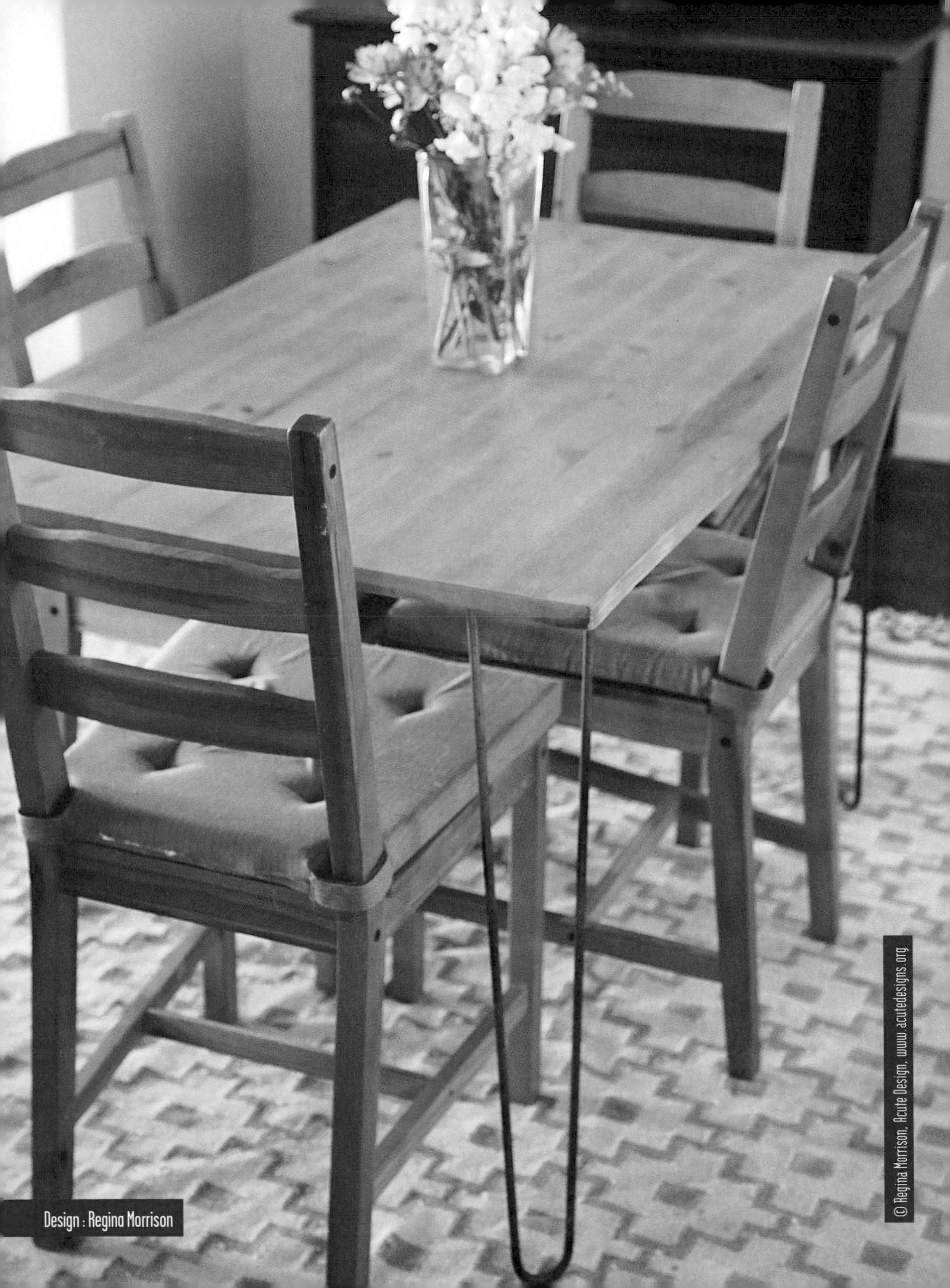

Design : Regina Morrison

SUPPOSE A PLATTER MARRIED A CACHEPOT

Photos : © Inter IKEA Systems B.U.

" The Hungarian lifestyle magazine Masni loves everyday objects that are easy to repurpose or adapt. This cake stand, for example, with its lacy pedestal and simple platform, combines the delicacy of a finely cut galvanized steel cachepot with the casual country look of a stoneware plate. With a little imagination, you can easily apply this idea to other utensils and tableware.

SUPPLIES

From IKEA:
- *Skurar* plant pot (4¾ in./12 cm diameter)
- *Arv* plate (11 in./28 cm diameter)

Other:
- Epoxy or strong all-purpose glue
- Permanent marker

TOOLS:
- Tape measure or ruler

HOW TO DO IT

1. Set the cachepot right side up on the back of the plate, using a tape measure or ruler to ensure that it is precisely centered. Mark its position with a permanent marker.

2. Apply a strip of glue to the bottom rim of the cachepot, where it will attach to the plate.

3. Position the cachepot carefully between the points you marked.

4. Set a pile of books on top of the assembly to apply pressure. Let the cake stand rest for at least 24 hours, until the glue is dried and fully set.

IT'S PERFECT FOR DISPLAYING YOUR BAKING TRIUMPHS!

A DESK FIT FOR A CHILD

Photos : © Inter IKEA Systems B.U.

> Some really great designs are a breeze to make. This is one of them. Cynthia Idels Hamelle took two chests, a plywood board, wall rails, and a few pegs, and figured out how to put them all together to bring order to the chaos of a child's room. Which will triumph in the end, organization or disarray? Impossible to say—but good furniture like this exists to accommodate life and all its unforeseeable events.

SUPPLIES

From IKEA:

• **Stuva 3-drawer chest**
• **Stuva 2-drawer chest**
• **2 PS 2014 wall rails or other similarly sized wall rails (46½ in./118 cm each)**
• **PS 2014 knobs (or other knobs of similar style) in assorted colors**

Other:

• **1 sheet of ¾-in. (2-cm) laminated plywood, 4 ft. x 8 ft. (120 cm x 240 cm)**
• **Decorative colored tape**

TOOLS:

• **Flat-head screwdriver**
• **Phillips-head screwdriver**
• **Drill**

HOW TO DO IT

1. Assemble the two *Stuva* units following the instructions provided.

2. Lay a piece of plywood cut to the width of the units and the desired desk length across the top of the units.

3. Decorate the exposed edges of the desktop with colored tape if desired.

4. Attach the *PS 2014* rails to the wall at the desired height above the desk. If you position the rails so they extend a little to the left and right of the work surface, you can hang bags and other long items on the ends.

5. Attach the knobs to the rails.

A CLEVERLY CONCEIVED DESK THAT LETS YOU STASH YOUR STUFF.

Design : Cynthia Idels Hamelle

KALLAX

EVERY WHICH WAY

KALLAX

Rekordit

The death knell has sounded again and again to mourn the passing of vinyl records, but they continue to hold their own in the world's increasingly digitized soundscape. Stylish and bold, album covers flaunt their graphic impact. Aficionados will applaud American designer Shane Keaney's Rekordit storage unit doors for showcasing these great works of art. Thanks to the removable panels in the doors, every cover can have its moment to shine.

SUPPLIES

From IKEA:
- **Kallax** 4-part shelving unit
- 4 **Gladsax** LP frames, glass removed
- 4 **Blankett** handles

Other:
- 4 piano hinges
- 16 flat-head screws
- 16 bolts, with nuts and washers

TOOLS:
- Pencil
- Sheet of cardboard
- Thumbtack or awl
- Repositionable tape
- Drill and drill bit suitable for use on aluminum
- Screwdriver
- Ratchet or a small adjustable wrench

YOU CAN MAKE THE DOORS FROM *GLADSAX* FRAMES.

1 Assemble the *Kallax* unit following the instructions provided.

HOW TO DO IT

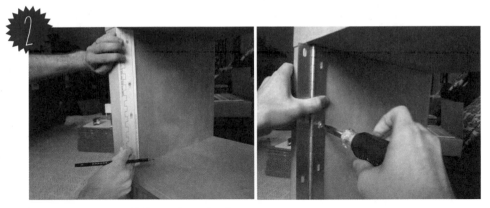

Position a hinge on the *Kallax* unit so that it opens on the side you prefer. Mark the position of the screw holes with an awl.

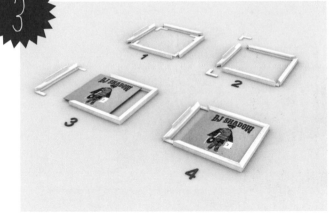

Assemble a frame and hold a hinge along one side. Mark the position of the holes. Set a handle on the opposite side of the frame and mark the position of the holes. Drill the marked holes in the *Kallax* unit and the frame. Attach the handle.

Attach the frame to the hinge using the nut and bolts. Screw the hinge to the *Kallax* unit. Select a cover to display and slide it into the frame.

Repeat the process to attach the remaining frames.

Design : Anna Pasco

KALLAX

A Retro Frame of Mind

The stylishly tapered lines of midcentury-modern furnishings were the forerunner of the IKEA style. Popular throughout the mid-twentieth-century, this furniture was the product of a booming standardized industrial process. It's an aesthetic that combines simplicity and functionality. Anna Pasco's design, which melds the midcentury style with a Kallax shelving unit, is an excellent example of this happy marriage.

HOW TO DO IT

1. Assemble the Kallax unit following the instructions provided.

2. Turn the shelf over and screw the wooden board to the bottom, taking care not to position the screws in the corners (where you are about to place the legs).

3. Mark the location of the legs on the board, using a ruler to make sure each is positioned the same distance from the edges.

4. Attach the legs to the board as required by the style of leg.

SUPPLIES

From IKEA:
• **Kallax 4-part shelving unit**

Other:
• **Plywood (⅝ in./1.5 cm) or wood board, cut to 29⅜ x 14⅜ in. (74.5 x 36.5 cm)**
• **Screws**
• **4 retro-style round or tapering table legs**

TOOLS:
• **Drill**
• **Screwdriver**
• **Pencil**
• **Tape measure or ruler**

KALLAX TAKES OFF WITH HIGH-STYLE CUSTOM LEGS.

Design : Agnes Hammar

© Photos : hejregina.elledecoration.se/Agnes Hammar

KALLAX

A Mobile Dressing Room

Every city-dweller is starved for storage and faces the challenge of finding additional space. It can be a costly project requiring custom-made installations. There is, however, another solution. You can adapt standardized furniture units to your apartment. That's exactly what Agnes Hammar did in her studio. It just took five *Kallax* shelving units with wheels and the application of a little elbow grease to solve her storage problems. This redesigned and improved storage space is compact enough to fit under a loft or any other nook available. Behind the sleek façade, simple shelves magically conjure all that clutter away.

WHITE WALLS CREATE THE IMPRESSION OF A LARGER SPACE.

SUPPLIES

From IKEA:
- *Kallax* 4-part shelving unit
- 4 *Rill* pivoting casters without locks

Other:
- Plywood (5/8 in./1.5 cm) or wood board, cut to 29 3/8 x 14 3/8 in. (74.5 x 36.5 cm)
- Screws and washers

TOOLS:
- Screwdriver
- Pencil
- Drill

HOW TO DO IT

1. Assemble the *Kallax* unit following the instructions provided.

2. Place the board in the center of the bottom of the unit and use a pencil to mark where you will attach it to the unit. (Avoid the corners, where you will need to attach the casters.) Drill holes at the marks and screw the board to the unit.

3. Position the casters on the board and mark the location of the screws using an awl or pencil, then screw on the casters.

level
MEDIUM

Photos : © Inter IKEA Systems B.V.

AN EVOLVING TABLE

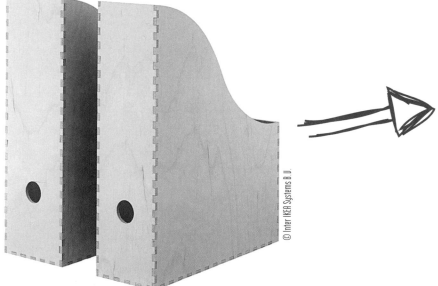

Design : Kenneth Yeoh

❝❞ The art of furnishing studio apartments can be summed up in just a few words: scale, multifunctionality, and mobility. This modular table designed by Kenneth Yeoh and constructed from *Knuff* magazine files offers all these features. Not even 2 feet (60 cm) wide, it's a clever addition to storage space, and its light structure makes it completely portable. Those tight on space and time will appreciate this table that's a snap to build and decorate.

AN IKEA ALTERNATIVE:
INSTEAD OF USING THE DRUMMER'S STOOL, YOU CAN USE IKEA'S *FROSTA* STOOL AND A *SNUDDA* LAZY SUSAN. FIRST GLUE THE MAGAZINE FILES TO THE LAZY SUSAN, THEN ATTACH THE LAZY SUZAN TO THE SEAT OF THE STOOL.

HOW TO DO IT

1. The base of this table is formed by four magazine files. Choose the shape you want for the table from the models pictured below and arrange the files accordingly. Glue them together one by one. Allow the glue to dry for 24 hours.

2. Remove the legs from the stool. Unscrew the seat. Mark the placement of the screws on the wooden board, and screw the board to the unattached metal frame to prepare the table's base.

3. Glue the files to the wooden board, and allow the glue to dry for 24 hours.

4. When dried, attach the table's base with screws to the stool frame. Your table is ready.

5. If you wish, you can give the table a decorative finish using paint or varnish.

SUPPLIES

From IKEA:
• 4 *Knuff* magazine files

Other:
• Wood glue
• Drummer's stool
• Wooden board (less than 30⁵⁄₁₆ in./77 cm square)
• Paint or varnish for decoration, if desired

TOOLS:
• Screwdriver

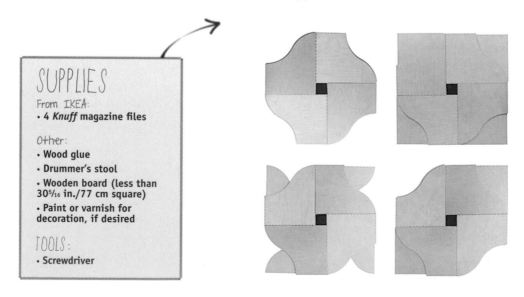

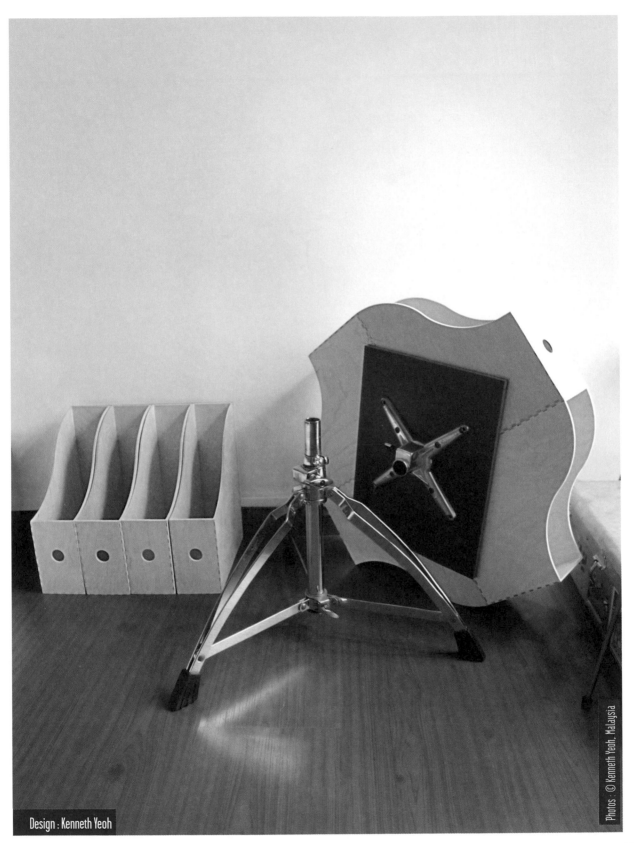

Design : Kenneth Yeoh

A LAMP THAT'S PRETTY AS A PICTURE

© Inter IKEA Systems B.V.

❝❝ Perfectly round, white, and ephemeral, IKEA's *Regolit* paper lantern has the timeless minimalism of classic design. This is a real plus for those who enjoy personalized treasures that can be crafted quickly and easily. With minimum effort, you can transform the lantern into a globe resplendent with lively illustrations. Marianne Norup selected nostalgic images from her childhood, such as rosy-cheeked youngsters, sprightly little fellows sporting train conductor outfits, and other characters from her favorite children's books. But there's nothing to stop you from creating your very own world!

HOW TO DO IT

1. Select your pictures. If you're looking for inspiration, consider cheerful illustrations from old children's books, brightly colored decorative wrapping paper, or nature books. In our example, the images were scanned and reproduced with a laser printer.

2. Decide on the size of the individual images. Here, they're 2½-in. (6.5-cm) squares, but of course they could be bigger.

3. Using a utility knife and metal ruler, cut out enough illustrations to cover the globe. (You'll need about 110 if you choose the same size images we did.)

4. Place the shade in a salad bowl to hold it steady, with the bottom facing toward you. Apply glue to the edges and backs of the illustrations and lightly press them onto the lamp, arranging them in a circle around the bottom of the sphere. Take care not to apply excessive pressure, and be sure to attach the images upside down. Continue until the first circular ring is complete.

5. Apply the next ring of images so that the new pictures only slightly overlap the first set, to avoid covering the images beneath. Wait for the glue to dry (about 30 minutes) between each ring.

6. Turn the shade over and glue on the remaining rings, attaching the images right side up. When the shade is entirely covered, let it dry at least overnight before hanging and lighting it.

Do not leave the lantern on while unattended.

SUPPLIES

From IKEA:
• *Regolit* paper lamp shade

Other:
• **About 110 pictures**
• **Laser or ink-jet printing paper**
• **LED lightbulb (emits less heat)**

TOOLS:
• **Color scanner and printer**
• **Utility knife**
• **Metal ruler**
• **Cutting mat**
• **Salad bowl**
• **Clear paper glue**

Design : Marianne Norup

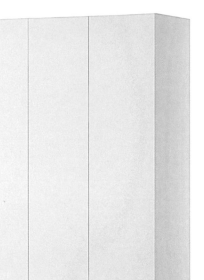

© Inter IKEA Systems B.V.

A TIMELESS ARMOIRE

 You could describe the *Pax* wardrobe as stark naked. It is devoid of moldings, ornamentation, and decorative touches. Impersonal, yes—but the design has its merits. It's very easy to embellish. The flat surface, uninterrupted by handles, gives free range to the imagination. It's a bit like the proverbial "little black dress" (another great classic that you'll want to stash in this armoire). It can be transformed at will depending on the circumstances or the season. Of course, you could stick some decorative trim on the front in a matter of seconds. But why not create a sensation? Ewa Pettersson's design, simply executed in permanent black marker, scales down the visual impact of the wardrobe's massive form and seems to round off its angular configuration. There's a pleasing irony in the way the austere twenty–first–century *Pax* embraces the flirtatious curves of the late–eighteenth–century Gustavian style.

HOW TO DO IT

1. Take a photograph of the armoire façade you want to reproduce.

2. If you're using a projector, draw the outlines on a transparency and project the image onto the Pax wardrobe centering the image.

3. Trace the lines with a permanent marker. If you are not using a projector, print out the photo and carefully draw the outlines on the armoire, closely following your sketch.

4. Allow to fully dry, and it's done!

SUPPLIES

From IKEA:
• White *Pax* 3-door wardrobe

Other:
• Black permanent marker (between 1 to 2 mm thick)

TOOLS:
• Overhead projector (if using)
• Inkjet printer with black ink
• Transparent film for overhead projector and printer

A PROJECTOR WILL MAKE THIS PROJECT MUCH EASIER TO TACKLE, BUT YOU CAN ALSO DRAW YOUR ARMOIRE FREEHAND, USING A PHOTOGRAPH AS YOUR GUIDE.

Design : Ewa Pettersson

CURTAINS WITH SUSPENDERS!

Amanda Kingloff figured out a way to liven up a window treatment using a Roman shade with some unusual accessories: suspenders. The *Annamoa* fabric she chose isn't available anymore, but of course you have no shortage of options—consider *Onskedröm, Doftranka,* and *Gitmaj,* for example.

© Inter IKEA Systems B.U.

HOW TO DO IT

1. If your window does not yet have a curtain rod, install one according to the package instructions.

2. Measure your window and add about 3 in. (8 cm) to the width and 6 in. (15 cm) to the height. Cut the fabric to these dimensions.

3. Fold over the sides and bottom about 1 in. (2.5 cm) and iron them down to mark where the hem will be. Slide a strip of iron-on tape into the fold and follow the instructions on the package to finish the hem.

4. At the top of the curtain, fold about 5 in. (13 cm) over and seal it with the iron-on tape, leaving space for the curtain rod to pass through.

5. Lay the curtain out flat on your work surface and decide how high the curtain will be when drawn. Mark the position of the buttons on the front. Decide how long you want the straps, adding 1 in. (2.5 cm), and cut them to length.

6. Pass the straps through the buckles, leaving enough of an overhang for a secure attachment. Attach with strong glue or sew together.

7. Sew the buttons on the front of the curtain, and then sew the ends of the straps directly behind them.

SUPPLIES

From IKEA:
- Curtain rod and related hardware, if needed
- Fabric of your choice

Other:
- Iron-on hemming tape
- 2 overall buckles
- 2 buttons
- 2 cloth straps wide enough to fit the buckles (1 in./2.5 cm wide)
- All-purpose glue, if needed

TOOLS:
- Screwdriver, if needed for curtain rod
- Measuring tape
- Scissors
- Iron
- Needle and thread

RECYCLE THOSE TODDLER OVERALLS WITH THEIR BUTTONS, BUCKLES, AND SUSPENDERS!

Design : Amanda Kingloff

THE TRAIN-TRACK TREE

 In this project, wooden train tracks are transformed into a tree to decorate a child's room. Make sure you don't run off the rails—lay out your design piece by piece on the floor before mounting it on the wall!

© Inter IKEA Systems B.V.

SUPPLIES

From IKEA:
- **Several *Lillabo* toy train rail sets (we used five)**

Other:
- **Polyurethane glue or construction adhesive**
- **Nonmarring tape**

HOW TO DO IT

1. Design the tree by laying out the tracks on the floor.

2. Glue the first piece to the wall, starting at the bottom (above the baseboard if there is one), and add the others one by one. Tape each piece in place with a nonmarring tape such as Frog Tape while the adhesive dries.

TOY TRAIN TRACKS
CAN TRANSFORM INTO
A GRACEFUL TREE.

Design : Mommo Design

A HELPFUL REMINDER

" Life sometimes feels like a runaway train, but the occasional reminder can steer you in the right direction. Whatever your destination, stay on track by playing with *Lillabo* and using the board for everyday reminders.

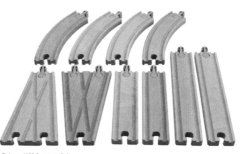

© Inter IKEA Systems B.V.

SUPPLIES

From IKEA:
- *Lillabo* toy train rail set

Other:
- Large piece heavy cardboard (we used 31½ x 47 in./80 cm x 120 cm, ⅛ in./3 mm thick)
- Pencil
- Fine sandpaper, if needed
- Black chalkboard paint
- All-purpose glue
- Fasteners appropriate for the wall surface

TOOLS:
- Wide-blade box cutter
- Mini paint roller or paintbrush
- Hammer

HOW TO DO IT

1. Working on the floor, lay the tracks out on the cardboard.

2. Trace the outline of the circuit with the pencil, then slide the tracks off the board so they retain their arrangement.

3. Cut the cardboard with a box cutter and, if necessary, smooth the edges with sandpaper.

3. Paint the cardboard with the chalkboard paint, using two coats and allowing time to dry in between. Allow the cardboard to dry completely.

5. Glue the tracks onto the cardboard, beginning at the intersection.

6. Allow the glue to dry for the recommended period before mounting the board on the wall, using fasteners appropriate for the wall.

THE LIGHT BOX

" Once upon a time, electricity was new and magical. It dazzled the eye in store windows and other privileged venues. Today the electric sign is commonplace in daily life. No longer perched on a public pedestal, it can spread the news at home as well as in the busy urban landscape. Our job is to choose the message.

© Inter IKEA Systems B.U.

SUPPLIES

From IKEA:
• *Ribba* frame of your choice, mat removed

Other:
• Polypropylene sheet, ivory colored (20 x 27½ in./50 x 70 cm)
• 9.8-ft. (3-m) self-adhesive LED strip lighting kit in warm white
• All-purpose glue
• White MDF panel, ⅛ in. (3 mm) thick, cut to the size of the frame
• Flat wooden letters of your choice
• Black spray paint
• Poster putty

TOOLS:

• Pencil
• Utility knife
• Cutting mat
• Wood saw
• Hammer

HOW TO DO IT

1. Lay the glass from the frame on the polypropylene sheet and trace its outline. Use a utility knife to cut the plastic sheet to size.

2. Replace the glass in the frame, lay the plastic sheet on the inner side of the glass, and restore the metal tacks that hold it in place.

3. Beginning at the lower-left-hand corner, attach the LED strip to the inside of the frame, following the contours of the corners closely. Remove the protective film from the adhesive gradually as you unroll the LED strip. Once the strip has been applied all the way around the frame, locate the closest "scissors" icon and cut. Attach the beginning and end of the strip with a dot of glue.

4. Using the saw, notch the lower-right corner of the MDF panel so the lighting cord can slide through. Put the panel back in the frame with the white side facing the glass.

5. Paint the letters black. Attach them to the outside of the glass with putty—this will allow you to change the message any time you wish.

Do not leave the light box on while unattended.

HELLO

ONE WORD SAYS IT ALL—AND LOTS MORE—WHEN DISPLAYED IN A LUMINOUS FRAME.

Design : Hëllø Blogzine

A STEP UP FOR GROWING GOURMANDS

❝❞ This stool is one of IKEA's best values. It's often used to give kids a boost at kitchen countertops. Here's a simple project that transforms it into a mini kitchen. Youngsters who love to act like grown-ups will be thrilled, because it puts everything at their fingertips.

Photos : © Inter IKEA Systems B.V.

SUPPLIES

From IKEA:
- *Bekväm* step stool
- *Bekväm* spice rack
- 2 *Ivar* hooks
- 3 *Losjön* knobs
- *Duktig* 5-piece kitchen utensil set
- *Grundtal* S-hooks
- Small kitchen items such as pots and dishware

Other:
- Black chalkboard paint
- Under-shelf-mounted wire basket
- Screws and anchors
- All-purpose glue
- White chalk marker

TOOLS:
- Paintbrush or mini roller
- Drill
- Measuring tape

HOW TO DO IT

1. Paint the top surfaces of the stool and the front rail of the spice rack with the chalkboard paint. Allow sufficient time for them to dry, then assemble the stool, following the instructions provided and mounting the hooks on the sides.

2. Mount the wire basket beneath the upper step of the stool.

3. Using a pencil, mark the placement of the knobs on the front of the upper step and attach them with glue.

4. Draw the burners with a chalk marker.

5. Attach the spice rack to the wall at the right height for your child, following the instructions provided. Embellish the setup by hanging the utensils from the S-hooks and adding other toy-size kitchen items.

KIDS WILL NOW HAVE
A PRETEND STOVE
SO THEY CAN COOK
LIKE MOM AND DAD.

Design : Mommo Design

© mommodesign.com

A CHILDREN'S WORKBENCH

❝❝ Who—or what—is *PS 2012*? Maybe a game console or a robot from that legendary interstellar saga? This enigmatic name originated with a simple coffee table introduced in 1995, the first piece in IKEA's *PS* line. Designer Ola Wihlborg declared that the world needed "things that move around," so she gave it wheels and rounded edges. That lightweight, nomadic table got a new look in 2012, and now Cecilia Thorsell has ingeniously repurposed the updated model, converting it into a workbench for children.

SUPPLIES

From IKEA:
- *PS 2012* **coffee table**

Other:
- **1 perforated hardboard panel cut to 27½ x 35½ in. (70 x 90 cm)**
- **Black paint or spray paint**
- **4 sheet-metal screws**
- **Pegboard hooks and other storage accessories**
- **Workbench accessories**

TOOLS:
- **Paintbrush or small roller, if needed**
- **Drill**
- **Screwdriver**

HOW TO DO IT

1. Paint the perforated panel black and allow it to dry.

2. Assemble the *PS 2012* table according to the instructions provided.

3. Drill four holes in the backside of the table. Attach the panel to the back of the table using sheet-metal screws.

4. Arrange and attach the hooks and accessories.

5. Place the workbench against a wall for added stability.

LOOK FOR TOOLS TO STOCK YOUR CHILD'S WORKBENCH AT TOYSHOPS AND CRAFT STORES.

Design : Cecilia Thorsell

COLOR SETS THE TONE

© Inter IKEA Systems B.V.

Need storage for several family members sharing a space so you can avoid stashing your beloved blankie on top of Dad's computer or your private diary with all Mom's stuff? The solution might be *Livet Hemma's* multicolor buffet, built from unfinished *Ivar* modules assembled as a unit. All you need to do to steer clear of trouble is establish a color code and let everyone select a favorite hue. Then everybody's secrets will be safe and sound.

SUPPLIES

From IKEA:
• 4 *Ivar* 2-door cabinets

Other:
• Primer for unfinished pine
• Acrylic paint in various colors
• Wood screws and fastening plates
• 1 custom-cut board to form the base (min. thickness 1¼ in./3 cm)
• 1 wooden board to form the top (approximately 11¾ x 126 in./30 x 320 cm)

TOOLS:
• Fine sandpaper
• Paintbrush
• Drill
• Screwdriver

THE NEUTRALITY OF RAW WOOD FREES UP THE IMAGINATION. LET EACH FAMILY MEMBER CHOOSE THEIR FAVORITE COLOR TO ASSURE FAMILY HARMONY.

HOW TO DO IT

1. Lightly sand the raw wood surfaces and wipe them clean.

2. Paint an undercoat using the primer. Allow sufficient time to dry, then apply the colored paints and let them dry.

3. Assemble the *Ivar* units following the instructions provided.

4. Attach the units together. First secure them to the base, and then to the wall, using the accessories provided.

5. Place the custom-cut board on top of the attached units to create a uniform surface.

Design : IKEA Livet Hemma

ORGANIZATION MAKES A HAPPY HOME

© Inter IKEA Systems B.V.

Rummaging through a closet is no fun. This design encourages disorganized kids to put things away neatly and where they belong. Plus, it's simple to make. The wall-mounted unit can be hung at just the right level for little fellows: not too high, not too low.

SUPPLIES

From IKEA:
- **1 or more *Ivar* 2-door cabinets**

Other:
- **Fine sandpaper**
- **Primer for unfinished pine**
- **Acrylic paint in various colors**
- **Masking tape**

TOOLS:
- **Pencil**
- **Paintbrush or mini roller**

HOW TO DO IT

1. Assemble the units, without the doors, following the instructions provided.

2. Sand the raw wood of the doors lightly and carefully wipe off the dust.

3. Mark the outlines of the doors and windows with adhesive masking tape. Then paint within the outlines, allowing sufficient time for the paint to dry. You can draw the outlines of the design before positioning the masking tape.

4. Repeat the process for the shapes of the roofs, protecting the outlines of the doors and windows, which must be thoroughly dry.

5. Attach the *Ivar* doors to the units.

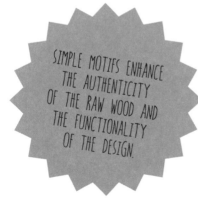

SIMPLE MOTIFS ENHANCE
THE AUTHENTICITY
OF THE RAW WOOD AND
THE FUNCTIONALITY
OF THE DESIGN.

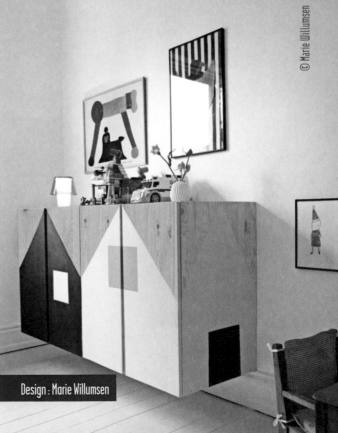

Design : Marie Willumsen

FAUX-MARBLE TABLE

The art of faux finishing lies somewhere between copying from life and wholesale creation. It's a painstaking task calling for lots of experimentation. You may have some false starts, but your time and patience will usually produce a stunning result. The faux marble finish on Danika Herrick's table is a good example.

CREATING A FAUX MARBLE EFFECT REQUIRES SOME TECHNICAL MASTERY. PRACTICE ON A SHEET OF CARDBOARD BEFORE BEGINNING THE PROJECT.

HOW TO DO IT

1 Sand the tabletop to slightly roughen the surface, then wipe off the sanded surface. Apply a coat of primer and allow the paint to dry. Sand again lightly and remove the dust before applying a second coat of primer. Allow the primer to dry according to the manufacturer's instructions.

Prepare one white and one gray glaze, following the manufacturer's instructions. To prepare the glaze, you can use a latex extender available in most paint stores, or a binding medium carried by craft supply shops. For both colors, use two parts binder for one part paint. The glaze should have the consistency of thick, whole milk.

Referring to your photograph of marble, use a pencil to sketch the veins of the marble on the tabletop.

2 Use a flat brush to cover a small area of the surface with white glaze.

3 Draw the veins with the gray glaze.

4 Dampen the sponge and gently wipe the surface, spreading part of the gray glaze and blurring some of the veins. Remember to work on only one portion of the surface at a time, and move quickly—the glaze dries fast.

6 Repeat steps 2 through 5 to make a second coat. For the second coat, divide the surface into different portions than you used for the first coat to prevent a patchwork-like surface.

Dip the feather in the gray glaze and draw it lightly over the whole tabletop, constantly moving it from left to right. Make thick veins following your pencil lines, blurring them with the shaving brush while they are still damp.

7

5 Next use the shaving brush and gently go over the surface to blur any lines or markings that are too distinct. Wipe the brush frequently to remove excess glaze. When you have finished glazing one portion of the tabletop, work on another spot until the surface is covered. Allow the first coat of glaze to dry. If some of the markings are still too pronounced, soften the effect with white glaze.

8

SUPPLIES

From IKEA:
• *Docksta* table

Other:
• White primer for unfinished wood
• Black and white acrylic or latex paint
• Latex extender
• Satin-finish transparent acrylic varnish

TOOLS:

• Fine sandpaper
• Flat paintbrush or small foam roller
• 2 bowls for the glaze
• Photo of the marble to be imitated
• Pencil
• Natural sponge
• Shaving brush or featheredge brush
• Feather
• Set of fine and medium paintbrushes, with rounded and slanted tips

Using the small brushes, add delicate veins and connect them with the larger ones. Once again, glide the brushes across the table's surface. Clean your brushes often; as the glaze dries on them, they won't work as well. When you are satisfied with the look of the surface, let the table dry completely.

9 Apply two or three coats of varnish to protect your creation.

THE JELLYFISH LAMP

© Inter IKEA Systems B.U.

❝❞ Jellyfish fascinate artists and designers, and they have inspired many extraordinary creations. Brenna Berger's lamp, created from IKEA's *Väte* pendant, has all the creature's grace and buoyancy. Its delicate paper streamers float in transient air currents, suggesting the sinuous dance of jellyfish tentacles, and its gentle glow conveys the magical translucence of these mysterious creatures.

SUPPLIES

From IKEA:
- *Väte* pendant lamp shade

Other:
- Blue tissue paper
- White tissue paper, preferably waxed
- Transparent paper glue
- Adhesive tape
- LED lightbulb (emits less heat)

TOOLS:
- Scissors
- Pencil

HOW TO DO IT

1. Assemble the lamp according to the instructions provided. Hang it at shoulder height so that you will be able to work comfortably.

2. To make the fringe on the bottom of the lamp, cut a long strip of blue tissue paper and fold it lengthwise. Make cuts through the folded edge about every ¼ in. (6 mm) to create a looped fringe. You may need to unfold and refold the cut strip to open up the loops a bit. Repeat until you have several strips of looped fringe. Glue them around the bottom of the lamp in several rows.

3. To make a tentacle, lightly sketch a circle between 6 and 8 in. (15 and 20 cm) in diameter on the white tissue paper. Cut out the circle, then start at the outside edge and cut the circle into a spiral. Make the beginning of the spiral rather wide and gradually taper the width as you cut toward the center of the circle.

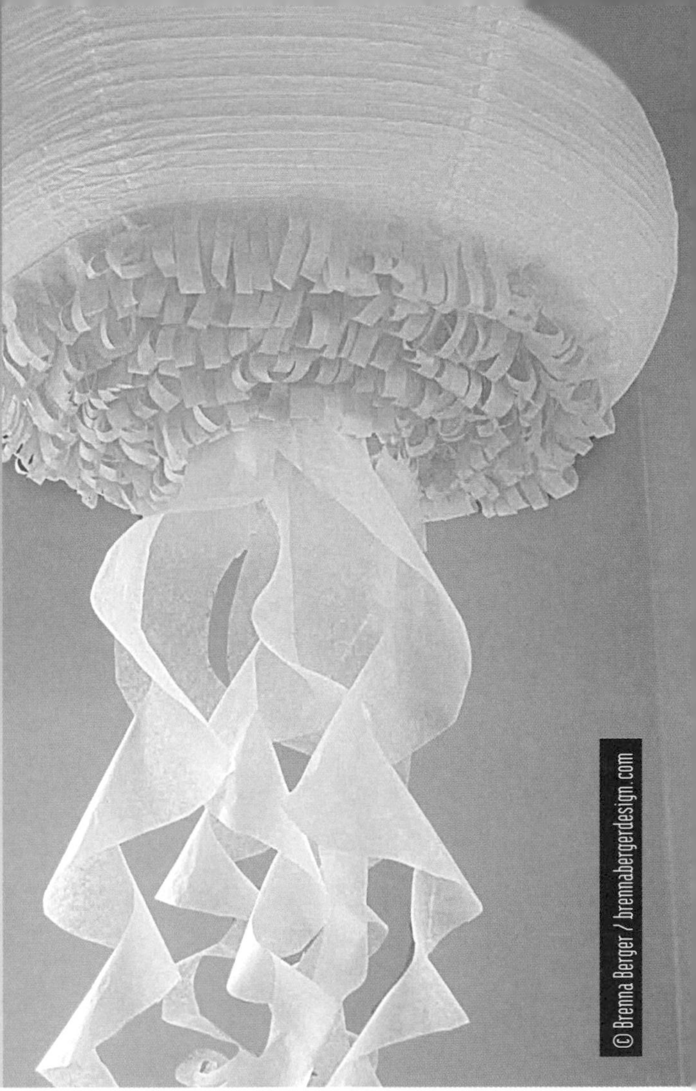

Design : Brenna Berger

4. Use tape or glue to attach the wider end of the spiral to the metal ring at the base of the shade and let the tentacle dangle free.

5. Repeat step 3 to make additional tentacles of different sizes by varying the size of the starting circles. Attach them to the ring, as well as to the transversal rod, as in step 4.

Do not leave the lamp on while unattended.

PIÑATA VERSION :

Select several different models of IKEA pendant lamp shades so you'll have a variety of shapes. Use multicolor paper and cover the shades completely with fringed paper strips (see step 2, opposite). Then use paper to close the hole in the bottom of the shade. Fill with candy, and you have a piñata!

HEADS OR TAILS SHELVING

© Inter IKEA Systems B.U.

In designer Francesco Pepa's opinion, "a library shelf is just a library shelf." And it's true that his creation is exactly that. But it's also a design with no real back or front. It's something like a palindrome: you can read it forward or backward. It has a recto and a verso, just like the books it's designed to hold. It's a clever sleight of hand. The library is playing a game of heads or tails, but it's really a very simple concept—the brackets are mounted on alternating sides of the shelves. It's a stylish statement that would have commanded the admiration of Ettore Sottsass and the Memphis Group back in the 1980s.

USE THE BRACKETS AS BOOKENDS.

SUPPLIES

From IKEA:

• 2 *Ekby Valter* tabletop brackets (or other bracket of similar style) for each level of a single-shelf unit
• *Ekby Valter* shelves or other similarly sized boards (47 x 11 in./119 x 28 cm)

Other:

• Metal paints in assorted colors
• 4 short furniture legs such as sofa legs for each segment of the shelf
• Screws

TOOLS:

• Fine sandpaper   • Screwdriver
• Paintbrush

HOW TO DO IT

1. Clean and lightly sand the brackets. Paint them and allow sufficient time to dry before assembling the shelves.

2. Attach the legs to the bottom shelf.

3. Assemble the shelves, placing a bracket at either end and alternating their placement front to back. You can create a variety of arrangements using this technique.

Design : Francesco Pepa

COOK UP A STYLISH
BLACK AND WHITE KITCHEN

Photos : © Inter IKEA Systems B.U.

Anna Krigh's DIY project is a clever take on the fun of playing house. Children love to imitate grown-ups; see how far their imagination takes them with this play kitchen. Just imagine all the appetizing meals they'll whip up.

SUPPLIES

From IKEA:
- Basic 2-compartment *Bestå* TV unit
- *Boholmen* single-bowl round sink
- *Sundsdvik* kitchen faucet
- *Lack* wall shelf of desired length
- *Bygel* rail
- 2 *Omlopp* round LED spotlights
- *Bygel* S-hooks
- 2 *Lappviken* doors
- *Duktig* 5-piece kitchen utensil set

- Small kitchen items such as pots and dishware

Other:
- Sheet of black adhesive plastic film
- White tape
- Double-sided tape or glue

TOOLS:
- Drill, jigsaw, and hole saw
- Screwdriver
- Compass or small plate
- Pencil
- Utility knife or scissors
- Roller
- Metal ruler

HOW TO DO IT

1. Before assembling the *Bestå* unit, mark the locations where you'll position the sink and faucet. Cut the holes for them with a jigsaw and hole saw mounted in a drill. Assemble the unit according to the manufacturer's instructions. Install the sink and faucet.

2. Cut the black plastic to a square the size you want to make your cooktop. Using a plate or compass and a pencil, draw four circles to make burners on the cooktop. Use the utility knife to carefully cut out the circles. Take each circular piece of plastic that you have removed and cut around the edge to make a smaller circle.

3. Attach the black plastic sheet for the cooktop to the surface of the chest. Attach the circles for the burners in the center of each cutout area.

4. Use white tape to make the details of the front of the stove. Use the utility knife to cut out strips for the oven door and control panel; add circles for control knobs; and cut out numbers to make the clock. Attach the tape to the door that will go beneath the cooktop and then install the doors, following the instructions provided.

5. Mount the shelf and the rail to the wall at desired heights, following the instructions provided. Attach the LED lights to the bottom of the shelf. Decorate the kitchen with utensils and kitchenware.

GRAPHIC WALL CLOCK

© Inter IKEA Systems B.V.

"It can be boring sitting across from a wall clock—staring at the time slowly ticking away. To alleviate the tedium of passing time, consider cheering up the clock face with an attractive design. It will set a rhythm for those passing quarter hours and liven up your day. All you need is a plain round wooden tray and a clockwork mechanism to transform the clock face's blank slate.

YOU CAN COUNT ON A BOLD GRAPHIC DESIGN TO JAZZ UP YOUR CLOCK FACE.

SUPPLIES

From IKEA:
- **PS 2014 round tray**

Other:
- **Colored paint**
- **Clock movement kit**
- **Decorative paper**
- **All-purpose glue**
- **Leather belt**
- **Nail**

TOOLS:
- **Large sheet of scrap paper**
- **Utility knife**
- **Flat paintbrush**
- **Pencil**
- **Gimlet or drill**
- **Hammer**

HOW TO DO IT

1. To protect the surface of the clock face, cut a circle of scrap paper the same diameter as the tray and press it onto the surface. Paint the rim of the tray any color you wish. Remove the scrap paper.

2. Use the utility knife to cut a quarter circle from the decorative paper to fit the clock face.

3. Use a pencil to mark the placement of your quarter circle and glue it onto the tray. (You could also paint a design directly onto the tray, if you wish.)

4. Make a hole in the center of the tray and insert the clockwork mechanism, following the package instructions and orienting the tray's handle at the twelve-o'clock position.

5. Cut a strip of leather from the middle of the belt. Discard the pierced and buckle ends. Slide the leather strap through the hole in the tray and join the two ends. Use the strap to hang the clock on the wall with a nail.

Design : Heju

FUN WITH *LACK*

© Inter IKEA Systems B.U.

These colorful tables will attract both young and old to gather around beloved board games—backgammon, Monopoly, checkers, Chinese checkers, and chess. The game board is an integral part of the table. It's a novel design that's both playful and decorative.

THIS DIY PROJECT WILL PROVIDE HOURS OF FAMILY FUN!

SUPPLIES

From *IKEA*:
• *Lack* side table in the color of your choice

Other:
• **Adhesive plastic film in the colors needed for the game board you've decided to make**
• **Game accessories (playing pieces, tokens, dice, miniature figures, etc.)**

TOOLS:
• **Picture of your game board for reference**
• **Pencil**
• **Utility knife**
• **Cutting mat**
• **Metal ruler**
• **Spray bottle filled with soapy water**
• **Roller**

HOW TO DO IT

1. Using your game board picture for reference, draw simplified versions of the board motifs on the back of the adhesive film. (Remember that they'll be reversed when you stick them on the table, so draw the mirror image of your desired result.)

2. Using a cutting mat, cut the motifs out with a utility knife.

3. Attach the pieces to the tabletop to make the board. After you remove the backing from each cutout, spray a little soapy water on the adhesive surface and the tabletop before setting it in place. That will enable you to move the shapes around to achieve the desired effect.

4. When the stickers are arranged to your liking, affix them using a roller (to squeeze the water out from underneath).

5. Assemble the table according to the instructions provided.

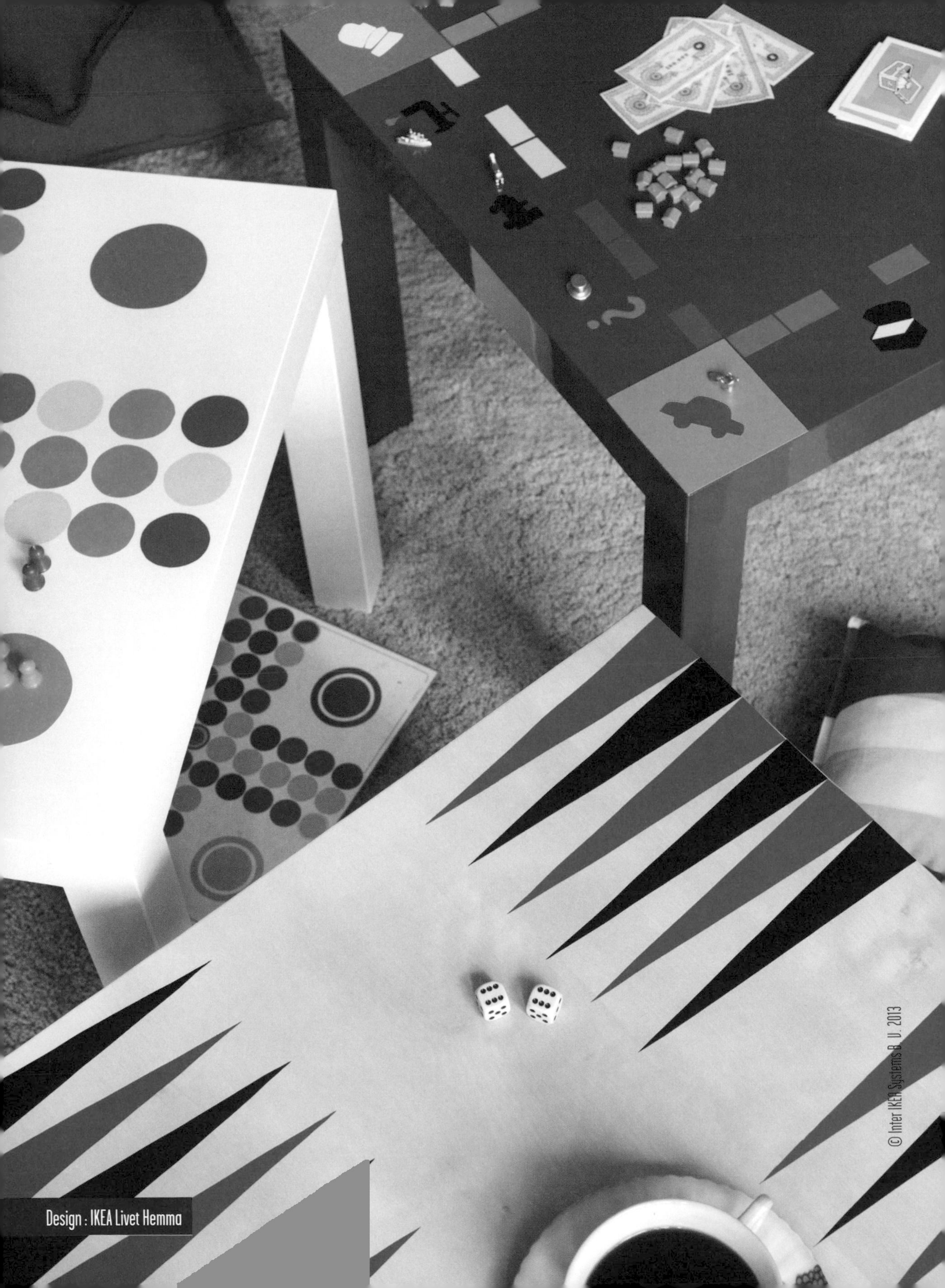

Design : IKEA Livet Hemma

THE ESPRESSO LAMP

Normal Arhitektura, an architectural firm in Sarajevo, has given a new look to the *PS Maskros* hanging lamp. It's an "espresso" makeover, crafted exclusively for the décor of a high-end café. The designers were after a distinctive look, with crisply delineated circular shadows projected onto the white walls. They couldn't achieve that effect with the delicate paper strands in the original lamp, so the firm simply replaced those with little white paper cups.

© Inter IKEA Systems B.V.

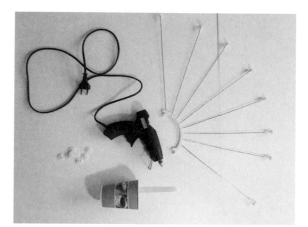

SUPPLIES

From IKEA:
- **PS Maskros pendant lamp in the desired size**

Other:
- **As many paper cups as arms on the lamp**
- **All-purpose glue sticks or liquid glue**
- **LED lightbulb (emits less heat)**

TOOLS:
- **Glue gun, if needed**

HOW TO DO IT

1. Assemble the framework of the lamp according to the instructions provided.

2. Glue the bottoms of the cups to the metal rods before snapping them onto the central support. Allow the glue to dry completely.

3. Use a transparent lightbulb, which will ensure that the shadows cast by the lamp are crisply delineated on the ceiling and walls. If you prefer a more diffuse lighting effect, use a frosted bulb. Use a licensed electrician to wire the lamp into the ceiling.

SUCCUMB TO THE TEMPTATION OF THE ESPRESSO LAMP!

Design : normal arhitektura

© www.normal.ba

THE GREAT WALL OF LEGO

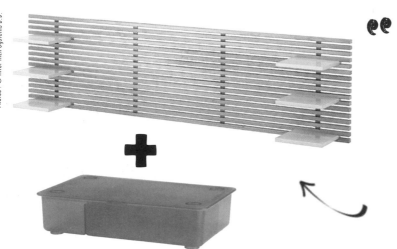

Photos : © Inter IKEA Systems B.U.

❞❞ Every Lego fanatic will eventually confront the thorny question of how to store all those blocks and accessories. A child may be perfectly capable of sorting them, but their storage requires some mature, astute analysis. Martin Storbeck has solved the problem by creating a vertical display case that doesn't require a single Lego block for its execution.

HOW TO DO IT

1. Assemble and attach the headboard to the wall according to the instructions provided. Do not attach the shelves that are included. They are not needed for this project.

2. Remove and set aside the lids from the boxes. Remove one of the U-shaped metal wire elements from each binder clip. Using pliers, open up a wire enough to slide it through the lid hinge of a *Glis* box. Pinch the wire back together and reinsert the ends into a binder clip using the pliers. Repeat to attach all the clips to the box hinges.

3. Install the boxes by clipping them to the slats of the headboard in whatever configuration you wish.

WHEN YOU'RE NOT PLAYING WITH YOUR LEGO BRICKS, YOU CAN COVER THE BOXES.

Design : Martin Storbeck

SWEET AND TART DOORMATS

© Inter IKEA Systems B.V.

❝❞ All too often, doormats are dingy black or brown, seemingly desperate to camouflage themselves. This project will have them flaunting lively pop art colors, so your front door will have a summery look all year round. It's an enticement to cross the threshold.

HOW TO DO IT

TO BEGIN:

1. Place a mat on kraft paper and trace its outline. Cut out three copies of this form to use as your stencils.

2. Place both mats on a plastic tarp and spray them with white paint. Let them dry. This will be the base coat.

TO MAKE THE WATERMELON SLICE:

1. Using one of the stencils, cut away and discard a 1¼-in. (3-cm) strip from the curved edge. Place the remaining semicircle onto the mat, aligning the straight edges, and weight it with coins to keep it in place. Spray the exposed edge of the mat with green paint. Set the stencil aside.

2. When the green paint has dried, take a second paper stencil and cut a 1½-in. (4-cm) strip from the curved edge. Save this strip and discard the semicircular piece.

3. Align the curved paper strip over the green paint (it will also cover a thin strip of white) and weight it down with

coins. Spray red paint over the exposed part of the mat, let it dry for 10 minutes, and repeat the process to ensure that the color adheres well. Allow the paint to dry, leaving the stencil protecting the edge in place on the mat.

4. Returning to the semicircular stencil that you set aside, draw the watermelon seeds as you want them and cut out the shapes. Lay the stencil over the red part of the mat and spray the exposed areas with black paint. Allow the mat to dry.

TO MAKE THE LEMON SLICE:

1. Spray the entire mat with yellow paint.

2. Using the stencil, cut off and save a 1¼-in. (3-cm) strip from the curved edge.

3. Align the strip on the curved edge of the mat, weighting it down with coins.

4. On the remaining part of the stencil, draw five lemon sections. Cut them out.

5. Arrange the five sections on the mat, weight them with coins, and spray the exposed areas with white paint. Allow the mat to dry.

Design : Brittany Watson Jepsen —thehousethatlarsbuilt.com

© Photos : Julia Lamotte

INVITE SUMMER TO COME KNOCKING AT YOUR DOOR— WOULD YOU PREFER WATERMELON JUICE OR LEMONADE?

SUPPLIES

From IKEA:
• 2 semicircular *Trampa* doormats

Other:
• White spray paint for the base coat
• Red, green, and black spray paints for the watermelon
• Yellow spray paint for the lemon

TOOLS:
• Kraft paper
• Marker, pencil, or chalk
• Scissors
• Plastic tarp to protect your work surfaces
• Ruler
• Coins

FROSTA

EVERY WHICH WAY

Design : Andreas Bhend

Wall-Climbing Shelves

The *Frosta* stackable stool is the essence of purist design—a bit featureless, perhaps. But use your imagination! Instead of assembling the parts into stools, why not think beyond those four legs and round top? Designer Andreas Bhend has used those simple elements right side up and upside down, inside the house and out in the snow, sliding, rolling . . . and even climbing the walls!

ANDREAS'S CREATIONS DESERVE YOUR ATTENTION—LIKE ALL IKEA PRODUCTS.

Photos and drawings © www.andreasbhend.ch

HOW TO DO IT

 Cut the stool seats in half to create semicircular shelves. (See Figure 1)

 To make a shelf that attaches at the center, cut a notch into the middle of a shelf's straight side. (See Figure 2)

 Decide how many left-facing shelves and how many right-facing shelves you want, and attach a leg to each shelf on the appropriate side. (See Figures 3 and 4)

 Attach one leg to the middle of the notched shelf, if you made one. (See Figure 5)

 Working on the floor, arrange the legs and the left- and right-facing shelves into the tree shape you want. (Not every leg you use has to be attached to a shelf, and you may wish to set one leg aside to mount on the front of the unit as a hat hook.) Drill pilot holes through the legs at regular intervals so you can screw the pieces together. (See Figure 6)

 Mount the assembly securely on the wall, using screws and anchors appropriate for your wall type. (See Figure 7)

 Screw the center-position shelf to the unit, fitting the notch over the central column. Attach the hat-hook leg above it.

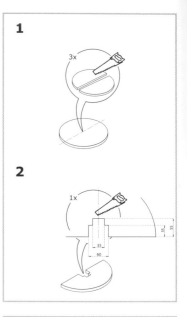

1

2

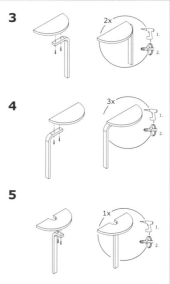

3

4

5

SUPPLIES

From IKEA:
- **3 *Frosta* stools**

Other:
- **36 wood screws**
- **Wall-mounting hardware appropriate for your walls**

Tools:
- **Saw**
- **Drill**
- **Screwdriver**

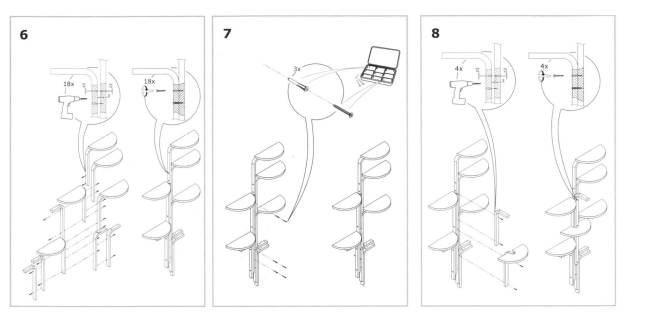

THE SHELVES HAVE A CENTRAL COLUMN COMPOSED OF LEGS FROM THE *FROSTA* STOOLS. FEEL FREE TO ADJUST THEIR ARRANGEMENT TO YOUR LIKING.

Design : Andreas Bhend and Samuel Bernier

FROSTA

The Sled

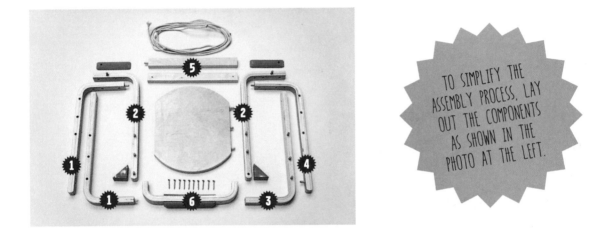

To simplify the assembly process, lay out the components as shown in the photo at the left.

SUPPLIES

From IKEA:
• 2 *Frosta* stools

Other:
• 10 wood screws
• 20 glue dowels, ¼ in. (6 mm) in diameter, 1¼ in. (3 cm) long
• Stickers or other items to add a personal touch to your sled. (Bhend customized his by printing out 3D parts at Le Fab Shop, www.lefabshop.fr.)
• Rope

TOOLS:
• Screwdriver
• Jigsaw
• Drill
• Clamp

Familiarize yourself with the instructions first, so you can position holes properly.

1. ON 2 LEGS (REFERRED TO BELOW AS "LEGS 1")

Drill three evenly spaced holes on the sides. Drill another hole at the top of each leg. Glue a dowel into the top hole.

2. ON 2 LEGS ("LEGS 2")

Drill three evenly spaced holes on the sides. These holes should be aligned with the holes on Legs 1. Drill another hole on the side at the top of the leg. Glue dowels into each hole on one leg. Leave the hole nearest the bottom of the other leg empty.

3. ON 1 LEG ("LEG 3")

Drill three evenly spaced holes on the sides. Glue dowels into each hole. Drill a hole at the top.

4. ON 1 LEG ("LEG 4")

Drill three evenly spaced holes on the sides.

Drill a fourth hole on the inner side of the leg. Glue in a dowel. Drill a fifth hole at the top. Glue in a dowel. The legs are ready to be attached.

HOW TO DO IT

1

Assemble four legs to create the sled's frame.

Legs 1 form the blades.

Attach them by laying them head to tail with Legs 3 and 4: one Leg 1 with the Leg 3 and one Leg 1 with the Leg 4.

Glue and secure them together with clamps until set.

2

Cut the edges of circular stool top to form two straight sides parallel to each other (ask a professional to make this cut if you are unable to). Drill three evenly spaced holes on each side.

Glue dowels in the right side.

Attach the seat to the frame. Put the Legs 1 and 3 components on the left and the Legs 1 and 4 components on the right.

3

Screw the two Leg 2s to the outside of the frame to form the front of the sled. (See photo at right. The transversal strips are installed following Step 4.)

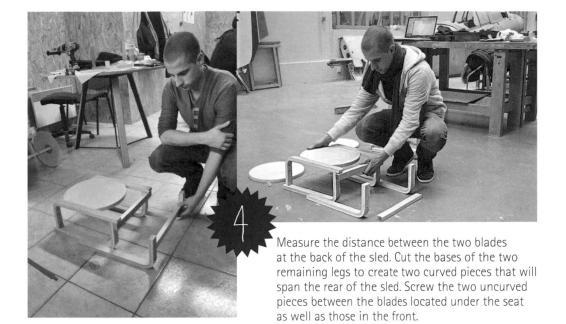

4 Measure the distance between the two blades at the back of the sled. Cut the bases of the two remaining legs to create two curved pieces that will span the rear of the sled. Screw the two uncurved pieces between the blades located under the seat as well as those in the front.

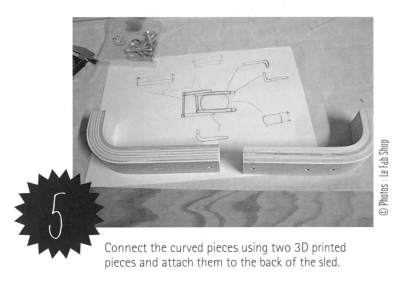

© Photos : Le Fab Shop

5 Connect the curved pieces using two 3D printed pieces and attach them to the back of the sled.

6 Reinforce the corners of the frame and the blades with 3D printed pieces.

7 Slide a rope through the pre-drilled holes of the *Frosta* stool legs.

Note: If you don't have access to a shop that makes 3D printed components, use metal connectors instead.

YOU'LL NEED TWO STOOLS TO MAKE THE BIKE.

Design: Andreas Bhend and Samuel Bernier

© photos : Le Fab Shop

FROSTA

An Old-Fashioned Dandy Horse

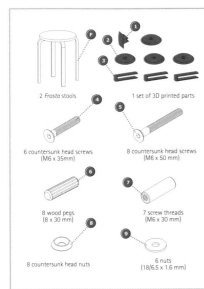

2 *Frosta* stools

1 set of 3D printed parts

6 countersunk head screws
(M6 x 35mm)

8 countersunk head screws
(M6 x 50 mm)

8 wood pegs
(8 x 30 mm)

7 screw threads
(M6 x 30 mm)

8 countersunk head nuts

6 nuts
(18/6.5 x 1.6 mm)

SUPPLIES

From IKEA:

• 2 *Frosta* stools

Other:

• 1 set of 3D printed pieces to be ordered from www.lefabshop.fr/fabstore or design your own
• 6 countersunk head screws (M6 x 35 mm)
• 8 countersunk head screws (M6 x 50 mm)
• 8 wood dowels (⅓ x 1¼ in./8 x 30 mm diameter)
• 7 screw threads (M6 x 30 mm)
• 8 countersunk head nuts (6.5 x 18 mm diameter)
• 6 nuts (18/6.5 x 1.6 mm diameter)

TOOLS:

• Jigsaw
• Drill

You will use eight of the two *Frosta* stools' legs; they will have holes drilled into them differently. The eight legs are numbered: F2, F4, F5, F6, F7 (x2), and F8 (x2). Pieces F1 and F3 are cut from the bases of Legs F2 and F4. They will be the movable attachment for the handlebars. See the drawing for Step 8 for the hole locations.

The seats of the stools will be used as wheels.

Give particular attention to assembling the frame and accurately locating the screws, pegs, and nuts to assure the toy's safety and stability.

HOW TO DO IT

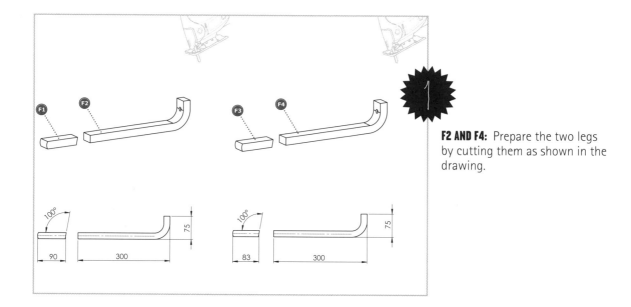

F2 AND F4: Prepare the two legs by cutting them as shown in the drawing.

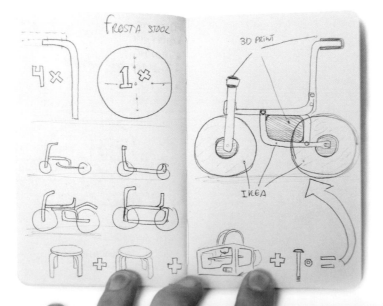

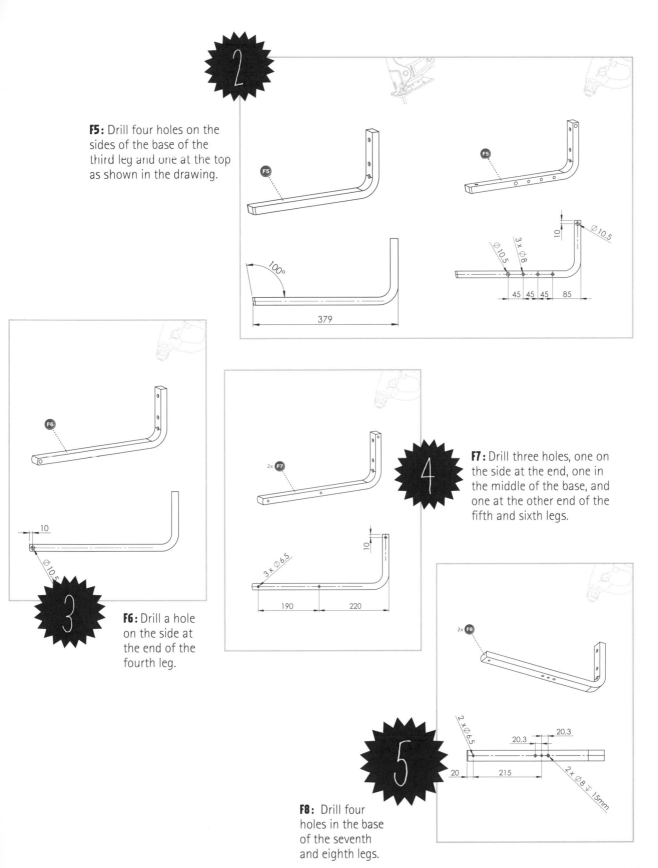

F5: Drill four holes on the sides of the base of the third leg and one at the top as shown in the drawing.

F6: Drill a hole on the side at the end of the fourth leg.

F7: Drill three holes, one on the side at the end, one in the middle of the base, and one at the other end of the fifth and sixth legs.

F8: Drill four holes in the base of the seventh and eighth legs.

An Old-Fashioned Dandy Horse

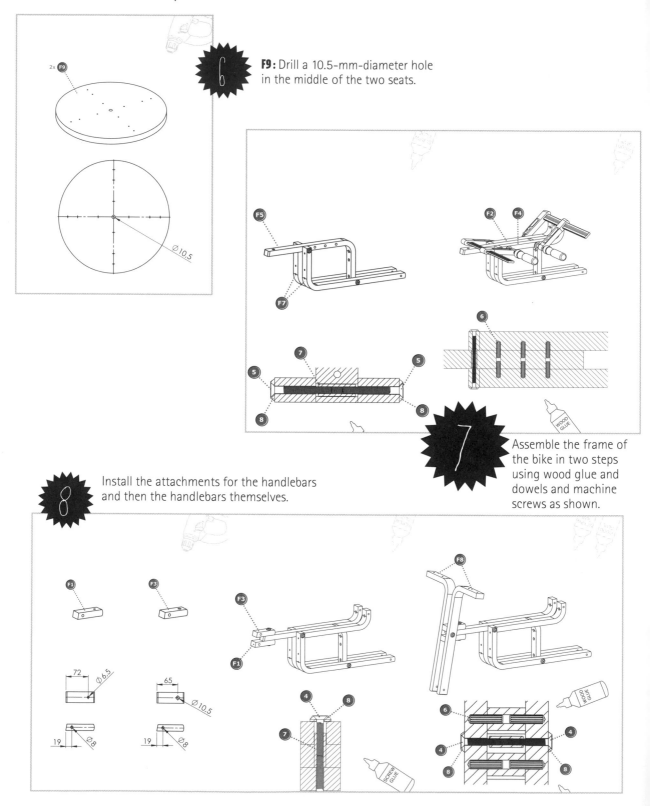

6 F9: Drill a 10.5-mm-diameter hole in the middle of the two seats.

7 Assemble the frame of the bike in two steps using wood glue and dowels and machine screws as shown.

8 Install the attachments for the handlebars and then the handlebars themselves.

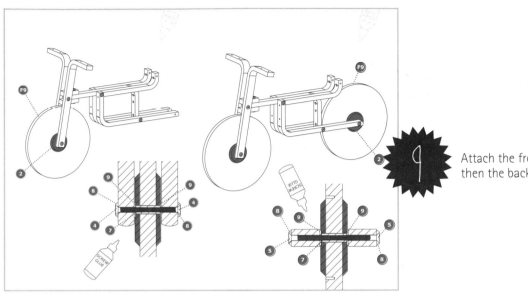

9

Attach the front wheel, then the back wheel.

10

Decorate and protect your new dandy horse with the 3D printed pieces.

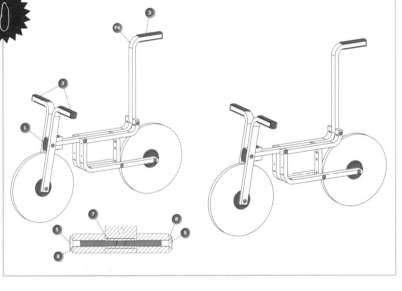

Note: If you don't have access to a shop that makes 3D printed components, use metal connectors instead.

Design : Maria Cañal Garcia

ALTERNATIVE:
LIKE MARIA CANAL,
OPT FOR A PILE
OF MAGAZINES TO
SUPPORT YOUR DESK.

Nico's New Desk

Nothing is better than just the right, ergonomically correct desk. For kids, this means it has to be the right height. And maybe just as important: It has to be wide enough and long enough to spread out on, to help them with both their schoolwork and creative art projects. Maria Cañal Garcia was looking for the perfect desk for her son Nico—so she designed it herself.

SUPPLIES

From IKEA:
- *Frosta* stool, legs only
- *Lillträsk* countertop

Other:
- **Screws**
- **1 wooden table leg**

TOOLS:
- **Awl**
- **Wood saw**
- **Screwdriver**
- **Drill**

HOW TO DO IT

1. Remove the legs from the *Frosta* stool. You will place one stool leg at each corner of the *Lillträsk* countertop to serve as desk legs. Using an awl, mark the position of the screw holes in the legs on the underside of the countertop.

2. Drill pilot holes in the countertop and attach the legs.

3. Cut the table leg to the same height as the desk. Attach it to the countertop at the center to provide additional support.

4. The desk is ready.

Design : Mommo Design

FROSTA

Frosta Swing

The back and forth motion of this charming garden swing seems rather unremarkable, but it will provide hours of fun for your swinging toddler.

ALWAYS FOLLOW CURRENT SAFETY RULES FOR SWING USE, ESPECIALLY SEAT HEIGHT. THE CHILD MUST BE ABLE TO GET OFF AND ON ALONE.

SUPPLIES

From IKEA:
• *Frosta* stool, top and 2 legs only

Other:
• **Paint for wood in desired colors**
• **Hemp or polypropylene swing rope (recommended diameter: ½ in./13 mm)**
• **Twine to wrap rope ends**

TOOLS:

• **Fine sandpaper**
• **Paintbrush**
• **Screwdriver**

• **Drill with bit the size of the rope's diameter**

HOW TO DO IT

1. Gently sand the wood, wipe it, and apply one or two coats of paint. Let the paint dry.

2. Screw the stool legs on opposite sides of the seat using the original holes and positioning the legs upside down.

3. Drill a hole in each leg large enough to pass the rope through, positioning it about 4 in. (10 cm) from the end.

4. Insert the rope through the holes and secure the ends using the twine, wrapping it tightly around the rope.

5. Install the swing from a sturdy doorway, horizontal beam, or tree branch (minimum diameter 8 in./20 cm) using a secure knot, such as a bowline.

level

ADVANCED

RECLAIMED WOOD BUFFET

© Inter IKEA Systems B.V.

Aniko Levai decided to pair this white cabinet with wood—not smooth, texture-free wood, but the raw wood used to make pallets. The result is a piece of furniture with a very distinct character and a classic design. It's an unusual duo but it works. The buffet wears its new exterior with pride.

HOW TO DO IT

EVEN THE HUMBLEST FURNITURE CAN HAVE CHARACTER.

1 Prepare your boards: Cut them to the size of the doors. Sand and finish them with walnut stain, following the manufacturer's instructions.

2 Clamp the pieces of wood to the doors, making sure the edges are aligned.

Drill through the back of the doors and partway into the boards (make sure not to drill all the way through—you don't want the screws to be visible). Screw the doors and boards together.

SUPPLIES

From IKEA:
• Basic *Bestå* TV unit in the desired size

Other:
• Enough wood boards (no thicker than ³⁄₈ in./1 cm) to cover the doors
• Walnut stain
• Wood screws
• Varnish, if desired

TOOLS:

• Saw
• Fine sandpaper
• Paintbrush
• Bar clamps
• Drill
• Screwdriver

3 Assemble the cabinet following the manufacturer's instructions. If desired, finish the doors by adding a coat of varnish to protect the wood.

A KITCHEN DRESSED IN BLACK

Photos : © Inter IKEA Systems B.U.

> Here's a modular kitchen with something unexpected. Today's kitchens are usually sleek and smooth—it's unusual to bring in raw materials like this barely sanded wood. The black stain brings out the knots and figure, and the result is surprisingly modern.

SUPPLIES

From IKEA:
- *Sektion* kitchen components
- *Ringhult* doors
- *Karlby* countertop
- *Fågleboda* handles

Other:
- Enough wood boards (no thicker than ⅜ in./1 cm) to cover all the doors of your components
- Black or dark walnut stain
- Screws
- Varnish

TOOLS:
- Saw
- Fine sandpaper
- Paintbrush
- Bar clamps
- Drill
- Screwdriver

HOW TO DO IT

1. Design your kitchen using *Sektion* components and *Ringhult* doors.

2. Cut the boards to the size of the buffet doors. Sand and stain the boards and the *Karlby* countertop, following the manufacturer's instructions. Allow them to dry.

3. Place the boards facedown on the floor. Position the doors on the boards, fronts against the boards.

4. Drill through the doors and partway into the boards (make sure not to drill all the way through—you don't want the screws to be visible). Screw the doors to the boards.

5. Finish the stained surfaces with varnish.

6. Install the *Sektion* components, the doors, countertop, and handles following the instructions provided with your design.

USE A BLACK OR DARK WALNUT STAIN FOR A SLEEK, MODERN KITCHEN.

Design: Benedikte Ugland and Linda Åhman

© photo : Anna Kern

THE REIMAGINED RAST DRESSER

© Inter IKEA Systems B.U.

" The small *Rast* dresser gets a makeover with this project. It loses its basic look and develops some character with two coats of varnish and a design that follows the wood-grain pattern of the dresser. With this new look, it's all dressed up and easily the centerpiece of any bedroom.

SUPPLIES

From IKEA:
- *Rast* 3-drawer chest

Other:
- Satin-finish white latex paint
- Thick permanent black marker

Tools:
- Hole saw, 2 or 2½ in. (5 or 6.5 cm) in diameter, and drill
- Medium and fine sandpaper
- Paintbrush or mini roller
- Tape measure
- Pencil

HOW TO DO IT

1. Using the hole saw, cut two holes in each drawer front to serve as the handles. Sand the cut edges with medium sandpaper, then sand the whole dresser with fine sandpaper. Wipe the surfaces clean.

2. Apply two coats of paint to the outside of all the dresser parts, allowing the required drying time in between coats. Let the second coat dry for one full day.

3. Using the pencil, trace the wood grain and knots you wish to reproduce on the fronts of the drawers. Have fun connecting the patterns of each drawer. Go over your pencil lines with the black marker.

4. Assemble the dresser, following the instructions provided.

Design : IKEA Livet Hemma

EMPHASIZE THE WOOD'S NATURAL TEXTURE BY TRACING ITS GRAIN AND KNOTS. THAT'S THE KEY TO CUSTOMIZING THIS BASIC PIECE.

THE LUXURY BATHROOM SINK

Like many inventive IKEA hackers, Annie Cournoyer is prepared to go all-out to achieve her vision. She devoted hours to working on this custom-made cabinet with handsome walnut trim. Underneath are big drawers to contain all the clutter that typically gathers around a bathroom sink.

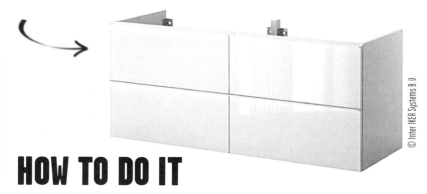

© Inter IKEA Systems B.U.

SUPPLIES

From IKEA:
- *Godmorgon Odensvik* sink cabinet with 2 or 4 drawers (originally meant for 2 sinks)
- Sink of your choice, with dimensions compatible with the *Godmorgon* cabinet
- Faucet of your choice

Other:
- Sheet of walnut veneer
- Plywood for the countertop
- 2 support brackets
- Stain, if desired
- Varnish
- Fine sandpaper

TOOLS:
- Drill
- Jigsaw
- Hammer
- Plumbing supplies
- Paintbrush and sponge brush for staining

HOW TO DO IT

1. Before assembling the *Godmorgon* components, cut out the interior walls adjoining the two compartments, leaving enough room for the plumbing.

2. Cut the plywood countertop to the dimensions of the cabinet.

3. Build a plywood box about 4 in. (10 cm) high to support the countertop.

4. Glue the walnut veneer to the countertop and its sides. If desired, stain the veneer, following the manufacturer's instructions. Apply at least two coats of varnish to protect the surfaces from water, following the manufacturer's instructions. Using the template that comes with the sink, lay out and cut the hole for the sink. Cut the hole for the faucet.

5. Install the brackets underneath the countertop to reinforce the structure. Attach the countertop.

6. Attach the cabinet to the wall with the appropriate fasteners, making sure the fasteners penetrate the wall framing. If you're not sure how to do this, consult a licensed professional. You may need a plumber to connect the faucet and sink.

A QUASI-CUSTOM FINISH FOR A BATHROOM UNIT.

Design : Annie Cournoyer

POLYLIGHTS

© Inter IKEA Systems B.V.

The five Platonic solids are the three-dimensional manifestations of regular polygons, and they are made up of four, six, eight, twelve, or twenty identical faces. These geometrical principles were certainly on Daniel P. Saakes's mind when he designed these lamps. With this project, six, twelve, or thirty-two *Lampan* lamps are assembled into perfect polyhedrons. These bright spheres, descendants of ancient mathematics, would have certainly pleased theoreticians who, through geometry and philosophy, searched for light.

Design : Daniel P. Saakes

© Daniel P. Saakes

HOW TO DO IT

FOR A SIX-LAMP POLYLIGHT

1 Cut the power cords off the lamps, leaving a 6-in. (15-cm) piece of the cord still attached. Set aside one of the power cords with its plug.

2 It is best to perform this step outside or with the window open because the burning plastic releases a strong odor. Spread the template out on your work surface and set a lamp on it. Mark the placement of the holes in the foot and cut them, using a soldering iron. Repeat for all the lamps.

3 Strip the plastic coating off the power cord on each of the six lamps.

Working with three lamps, connect the brown wires to one connector and the blue wires to another one. Repeat the process with the three other lamps. You'll end up with four cables (two brown and two blue).

Using the last wire connector, connect all the blue cables together and all the brown cables together. Attach these connectors to the corresponding wires on the power cord you set aside.

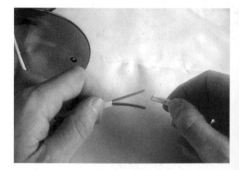

4 Bind the lamps together, attaching the cable ties through the holes you made so that the feet of the lamps form the sides of a polyhedron.

5 Use a licensed electrician if you wish to wire the lamp to the ceiling.

If you are not comfortable with basic wiring, ask an electrician to make the connections.

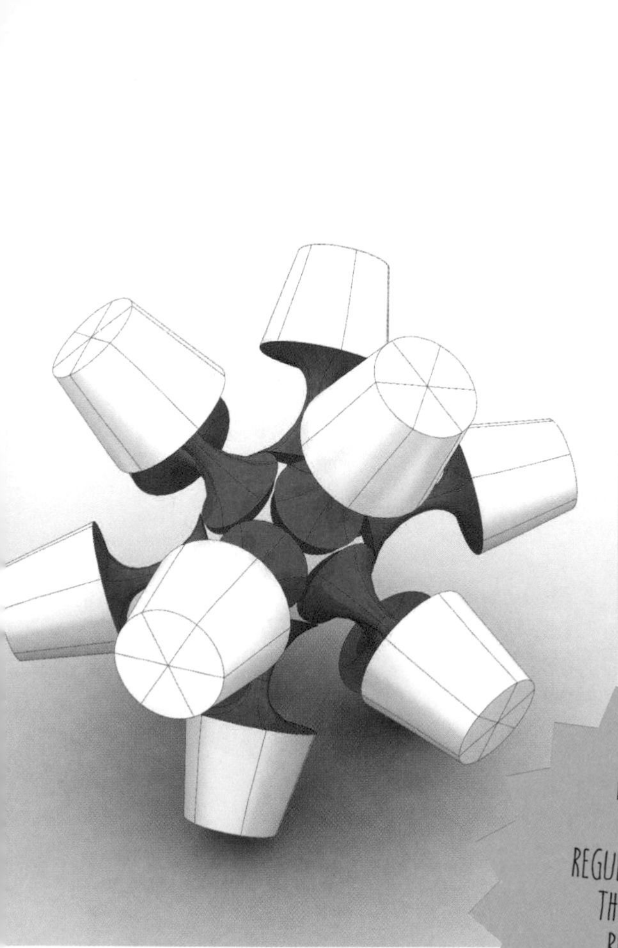

FOR YOUR SAFETY,
FOLLOW WIRING
REGULATIONS AND FOLLOW
THE MANUFACTURER'S
RECOMMENDATIONS
REGARDING BULB WATTAGE.

SUPPLIES

From IKEA:
- 6 *Lampan* table lamps

Other:
- Wire connectors
- Pack of electrical cable ties

TOOLS:

- Wire cutters
- Template for 6-lamp Multilight (www.
instructables.com/id/Big-lamps-from-
Ikea-lampan-lamps)
- Permanent marker
- Scissors
- Ruler
- Soldering iron
- Stripping pliers
- Crimping pliers

Note: Daniel P. Saakes devised templates
for using six, twelve, and thirty-two
lamps. For more information, visit
saakes.net/projects/lampan.

FARMHOUSE TABLE

Design : Monica Mangin

We've all seen pictures of those idyllic country meals spread out over long, rustic farm tables. Those tables were the standard in the past, but now they are rare. New ones are expensive. To bring everyone together without going broke, you can take two of the best-priced tables from IKEA and give them a raw wood top. Let the fun begin!

HOW TO DO IT

ADD CHARACTER TO YOUR DINING ROOM BY TRANSFORMING PLAIN WOODEN TABLES.

1

Join the two tables by placing one of the 1 x 2-in. (22 x 57-mm) boards over the seam and screwing it down.

2

To complete the support framework for the expanded tabletop, arrange the remaining eight boards so they are evenly spaced across the table and aligned at the edges. Screw the lumber directly onto the tabletop (three screws per piece of lumber should be enough).

3

Cut the long 8-in. (20-cm) -wide boards that will become the tabletop to their precise size. When you determine the length of these boards, take into consideration that one of the shorter 8-in. (20-cm) -wide boards will be placed perpendicularly at each end. Sand all the tabletop boards, rounding the corners as a finishing touch.

5 To make the table apron, measure and cut the 1 x 3-in. (28 x 67-mm) lumber and attach it to the framework under the boards.

Place the boards into the desired configuration. Attach them from underneath the table using screws long enough to go through the support framework and the tabletop boards without coming through to the surface.

4

© Photos : Monica Mangin / East Coast Creative

6 Optional: To give the wood an aged look, stain it, then distress the surface with screw heads, a piece of brick, or a length of chain (practice on scrap wood first).

7 To finish, apply two or three coats of polyurethane.

SUPPLIES

From IKEA:
• 2 *Ingo* tables

Other:
• 1 x 2-in. (22 x 57-mm) lumber:
  - 9 pieces cut to 3¾ ft. (1.2 m)
• 8-in. (20-cm) -wide wood boards for the tabletop:
  - 6 pieces 8 ft. (243 cm) long
  - 2 pieces 4 ft. (122 cm) long
• 1 x 3-in. (28 x 67-mm) lumber:
  - 2 pieces cut about 31½ in. (80 cm)
  - 2 pieces cut about 94½ in. (240 cm)
• Walnut stain or other finish
• Polyurethane varnish
• Screws

TOOLS:
• Drill
• Screwdriver
• Tape measure
• Pencil
• Saw
• Sandpaper
• Paintbrushes
• Brick or chain (optional)

THE MODULAR BOOKSHELF AND DESK

© Inter IKEA Systems B.U.

In this project, *Trofast* storage bins are no longer just bins; they're also shelving and light filters. Arranged in a honeycomb pattern, they become a modular bookshelf that runs up the wall, as well as a desk. These pieces create a uniform and modern space. As practical as it is original, this assemblage even involves a few surprises—to start, going into an IKEA to purchase nearly one hundred bins at once!

HOW TO DO IT

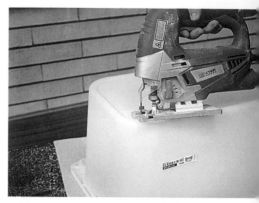

 Using a jigsaw, cut off the bottoms of as many of the taller *Trofast* bins as you want for wall-mounted shelves. Sand the raw edges using a palm sander.

 Plan the configuration you want and mark where on the wall you will place both the open bins (for shelves) and intact bins (for lights).

 Place the *Dioder* light strips where desired. Mount the bins on the wall, according to your plan, using the appropriate hardware.

 To create the light ceiling, attach the LED adhesive strips, then mount rows of the shallow bins over them.

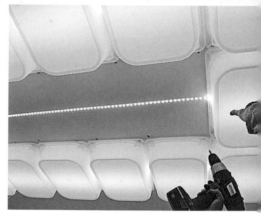

 The desk is made by turning the Torsby tables on their sides. Place them next to each other then attach light strips and the bins to the vertical surface (see diagram). Attach the plywood to the horizontal legs to create a work surface. If desired, you can even add a custom glass compartment on top like the designer of this desk. Either way—don't forget to use the bins inside the desk like drawers!

SUPPLIES

From IKEA:

- 9-in. (23-cm) deep *Trofast* bins, for bookshelves
- 4-in. (10-cm) deep *Trofast* bins, for the desk and ceiling lights
- *Dioder* LED light strips (one per bin)
- 2 *Torsby* tables

Other:

- Screws and anchors appropriate

for your walls

- Sheet of ¾-in. (2-cm) -thick plywood or melamine
- Custom glass compartment (optional)

TOOLS:

- Jigsaw
- Fine sandpaper
- Palm sander or sanding block
- Drill
- Screwdriver
- Tape measure
- Pencil

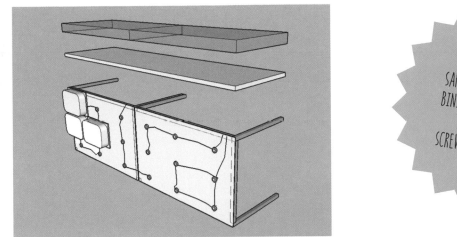

FOR ADDITIONAL SAFETY THE BOOKSHELF BINS CAN BE ATTACHED TO WOOD SLATS SCREWED TO THE WALL.

© Photos : mommadesign.com

A CEILING SPIDER

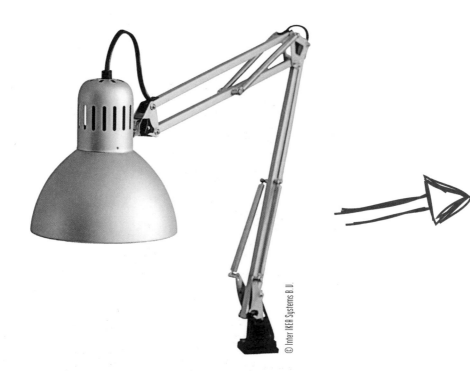

© Inter IKEA Systems B.V.

Design : Uber Design House

❝ It's like a spider hanging from the ceiling! Around its belly, long legs perfectly light the room and can be angled as needed. There's never been such a compliant spider, but it's important to keep it a bit wild and make it your own. There will always be eight legs of course!

HOW TO DO IT

1 Attach the *Tertial* lamp bases to the round base. Drill three evenly spaced holes for the threaded rods about midway between the center and the edge of the base.

SUPPLIES

From IKEA:
• **8 *Tertial* lamps**

Other:
• **1 wooden round board 4 ft. (122 cm) in diameter, painted black or desired color**
• **3 threaded rods of your desired length (take the height of your ceiling into account, and for your safety, leave a large amount of space between the ceiling and the bulbs)**
• **Nuts and washers**
• **Screws to attach lamps to base**
• **Terminal block**
• **Electrical wire**

TOOLS:
• **Drill**
• **Screwdriver**
• **Tape measure**
• **Pencil**

2 Attach the threaded rod to the ceiling in the same pattern as the holes in the round base. The rods should be connected to a structural component, not just drywall or plaster. If you're not sure how to do this, consult someone who is.

4

Thread the rods through the base and secure them using the nuts and washers. Connect the main wire to the terminal block.

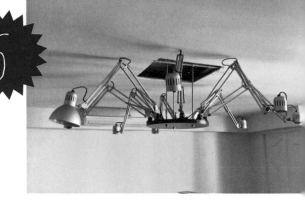

5

Use a licensed electrician to wire the fixture into the ceiling.

3

Cut the power cord on each lamp above the switch. Strip the wires and connect them to a terminal block, following the manufacturer's safety rules and regulations.

If you are not comfortable with basic wiring, ask an electrician to make the connection.

ONCE YOU DECIDE ON THE CONCEPT, YOU CAN CUT THE RODS TO ADJUST TO YOUR DESIRED HEIGHT.

THE SEWING TABLE

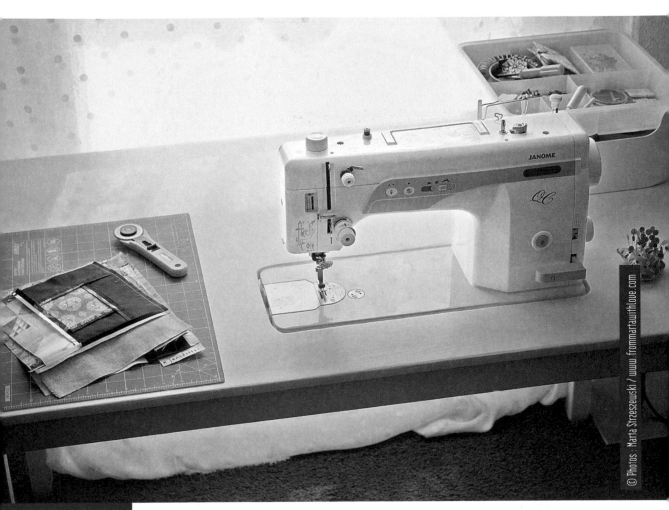

Design : Marta Strzeszewski

 This idea is beautifully simple—embedding a sewing machine into a table—but in fact, the steps required to achieve it are rather complex. Think of the instructions described on the following spread like a pattern, and make this your own using your particular skills and furniture.

HOW TO DO IT

1 Assemble your table according to the instructions provided and then decide on the placement of the machine. Measure the base of your sewing machine and make a corresponding template from cardboard or paper. Trace the outline of the template on the top and cut the hole with a jigsaw.

2 Remove the tabletop from the assembly, leaving the feet and framework together.

Along the width of the framework, attach two wood brackets, one on either side of the hole. You can reinforce this second framework using braces.

Drill four holes into these braces. Insert the bolts. Hang the support board from the braces using nuts and washers. The structure must be solid enough to bear the weight of the machine and the vibrations it will make when in use.

Reattach the tabletop to the framework.

USE A DRILL GUIDE AND A COUNTERSINK, AND YOUR TABLE WILL LOOK PERFECT!

 Paint the wood, or if desired, give the wood a patina. Protect the tabletop with varnish.

When your table is ready, make sure everything is in place: Slide the electrical cords in the space left between the tabletop and the support board. Place your machine into the tabletop and tighten or loosen the nuts until the machine base is level with the tabletop. Cover the ends of the bolts with protection caps so you won't scrape your knees.

For more information, see http:// frommartawithlove.com/2012/10/diy-ikea- sewing-table-tutorial.

SUPPLIES

From IKEA:
- *Ingo* table

Other:
- Support board, at least 2 in. (5 cm) longer and wider than your sewing machine base
- 2 x 2-in. (5 x 5-cm) board at least twice as long as the width of the table for braces
- 4 wood screws or brackets to secure braces
- 4 bolts (4 in. long x ¼ in. diameter) with bolt caps, 8 washers, and 8 nuts
- Paint or stain, if desired
- Polyurethane varnish

TOOLS:
- Protective glasses
- Jigsaw
- Drill
- Screwdriver
- Tape measure
- Pencil
- Paintbrush

HANDCRAFTED SHELVES

© Inter IKEA Systems B.V.

" A simple metal bookshelf is a blank slate, just waiting to be transformed. The regularity and uniformity of its standardized shape can turn out to be the ideal basis for an original creation. That's what happened when Soffia Gardarsdottir wanted a bookshelf with a handcrafted aesthetic, and in the end, she created a piece of furniture that transformed her living room.

HOW TO DO IT

Cut the bottom of the metal posts for the shelving units to the desired height. Make sure you don't cut the premade holes at the top end of the posts.

Apply the spray paint to the separate parts of the shelves. Allow them to dry and then apply the transparent finish.

The posts have four holes along what is intended to be the upper portion so that the height of the upper shelves can be adjusted. By flipping the posts over, you can place the lower shelf a few inches off the floor. That's what the designer did for this DIY project.

Flip the posts if desired, then assemble the shelves following the instructions provided.

Arrange the shelving units where you want them. Cut the wood boards to your desired length, then mark the positions of the shelf posts on each board and cut notches so that the board will fit around the posts. Sand, then stain the boards.

When installing the wood shelves, if the paint on the metal posts chips, use a small brush to touch up.

Insert the wood shelves into the *Hyllis* units.

SUPPLIES

From IKEA:
- 4 *Hyllis* shelving units

Other:
- Black spray paint for metal
- Transparent varnish spray
- 12-in. (30.5-cm) -wide board (for the top shelf)
- 10-in. (25-cm) -wide boards (for the bottom shelves)
- Fine sandpaper
- Wood stain of your choice (Soffia mixed old oak and teak)
- Small paintbrush for touchup

TOOLS:
- Measuring tape
- Hacksaw
- Screwdriver
- Saw
- Pencil

A KITCHEN ISLAND

Design : Danny Cerezo

A kitchen island is a special treat for homeowners—even a luxury. By using only the *Malm* dresser and IKEA countertops, Danny Cerezo's family cooked up an island at a low cost. And they burned a few calories while making it.

HOW TO DO IT

1 Using tape, mark out the footprint of the base on the floor (63 x 24 in./160 x 60 cm).

4 Adjust the *Sektion* cabinet so that it is the same height as the dresser and assemble it according to the instructions.

2 Build a frame of that size with the 2x4s, using the metal braces to secure the corners. Brace the frame by attaching a fifth piece of lumber across the width.

3 Assemble the dresser, following the instructions provided, and then place it on the base, facing in the direction where you want the drawers, its side aligned with a short edge of the frame. If you like, attach it to the frame using two straight brackets.

6 Cut one of the worktops into two pieces sized to fit on either end of the island. Cut the second worktop, if needed, to fit on the top. Using angle brackets, attach the end pieces and the countertop to the island.

5 Place the cabinet on the base next to the dresser, with its back and side aligned with the corner of the base frame. If you like, attach it to the frame using two straight brackets. You can reinforce it by screwing it to the dresser.

7 Cut the plywood to size and mount it on the back of the *Sektion* cabinet and the base frame using heavy-duty adhesive. You can either paint the plywood surface or cover it with a sheet of vinyl wall panel. Once the island has been assembled, lightly sand the countertop and sides. Finish the surfaces with food-safe butcher block oil or food-safe varnish.

NOTE: TO MAKE THE PROJECT EASIER, WE'VE ADAPTED THIS PIECE TO THE STANDARD DIMENSIONS OF IKEA FURNITURE.

SUPPLIES

From IKEA:

- **3-drawer *Malm* dresser (31½ x 18⅞ x 30¾ in./80 x 48 x 78 cm)**
- ***Sektion* base cabinet frame (30 x 24 x 30 in./76.2 x 61 x 76.2 cm)**
- **2 *Karlby* kitchen worktops**
- **Recommendation: For the base cabinet, check out the "as-is" section. That's where discontinued items are on sale.**

Other:

- **2 x 4-in. (5 x 10-cm) lumber (You'll need about three of the standard 8 ft./244-cm boards.)**
- **8 corner braces and screws**
- **4 straight brackets**

- **Sheet of plywood large enough to serve as the facing**
- **Construction adhesive**
- **Paint, if desired**
- **Sheet of vinyl wall covering and acrylic glue, if desired**
- **Food-safe butcher block oil or polyurethane varnish**

TOOLS:

- **Masking tape**
- **Measuring tape**
- **Saw**
- **Drill**
- **Screwdriver**
- **Paintbrush, if needed**
- **Fine sandpaper**
- **Palm sander**

ROBIN HOOD'S CROSSBOW

Designer Kieren Jones's crossbow looks like it came straight out of a tale of chivalry. But with this crossbow there's no fighting with thieves or robbing rich lords—and there are no tournaments. This crossbow is harmless.

© Inter IKEA Systems B.V.

SUPPLIES

From IKEA:
- 2 *Bumerang* hangers
- 3 *Ralta* hangers (or wooden hangers of a similar style)

Other:
- Tape
- Wood glue
- Dowels
- Fine sandpaper
- Thin cord

TOOLS:
- Drill
- Hammer
- Tape measure
- Pencil
- Saw

HOW TO DO IT

1. Remove the rods from the two *Bumerang* hangers.

2. Unscrew the hooks from the three *Ralta* hangers, and separate the two "shoulders" from each hanger.

3. To make the crossbow handle, glue the flat sides of two shoulders together head-to-tail. Hold the pieces together with tape until the glue dries.

4. Take another shoulder, and glue the two *Bumerang* rods to the straight side. Hold the pieces together with tape until the glue dries.

5. To form the bow, attach a shoulder on each side of the crossbow body by inserting dowels into aligning holes. Glue the dowels in place.

6. Attach the body to the handle with a short length of rod from a *Bumerang* hanger.

7. To string the crossbow, cut two slits on the ends of the shoulders and string the thin cord through the slits. Knot the ends of the cord.

KIEREN JONES IS A DESIGNER AND INVENTOR WHO WORKS ON SMALL-SCALE ARCHITECTURE AND DESIGN PROJECTS THAT RESPOND TO THE ENVIRONMENT AROUND HIM. HIS WORK EXPLORES THE CONNECTION BETWEEN AMATEUR CRAFTSMEN AND INDUSTRIAL MANUFACTURERS.

FLAT PACK REARRANGED

STRUM

Design : Kieren Jones

A STAG'S HEAD HANGING TROPHY

> The deer need not fear the crossbow. Elegant and distinguished, he stands like a trophy to forest creatures.

© Inter IKEA Systems B.U.

SUPPLIES

From IKEA:
- **2 *Ralta* hangers (or wooden hangers of a similar style)**
- **6 *Bumerang* hangers**

Other:
- **Wood glue**
- **Tape**
- **Nails**
- **Fine sandpaper**
- **Screws to attach to wall**

TOOLS:
- **Saw**
- **Pencil**
- **Tape measure**
- **Drill**
- **Hammer**

HOW TO DO IT

1. First, unscrew the hooks from the *Ralta* hangers and separate each into "shoulders." Cut the wider side of two shoulders at an angle, then measure and mark 5 in. (12 cm) from the wide edge on each shoulder and cut on an angle. Glue the two pieces together along their long, straight sides to form the head of the animal. Tape together and allow the glue to dry.

2. Cut the two remaining shoulders on an angle, and position one on each side of the head. They should stick out beyond the sides of the head.

3. Detach the horizontal rods of the *Bumerang* hangers. Glue one rod along the flat edge of each of the shoulders that will form the top of the head. Tape the pieces together while the glue dries.

4. Glue this structure to the top of the animal head. Tape the pieces together until the glue dries.

5. Cut the remaining rods into different sizes and compose the antlers, gluing and nailing the pieces to the head.

6. Mark the eyes and nostrils and then drill four holes. Use these holes to attach the trophy to the wall.

THE HANGER
HUNT IS ON!

FLAT PACK
REARRANGED

TROPHI

KURA
EVERY WHICH WAY

FLYER

LION

Design : Emma Silver

KURA

Kura Transformed

With only a few rolls of wallpaper, Emma Silver makes the bulk of the *Kura* bed disappear, transforming it into more than just a piece of furniture. Using wallpaper that matches the walls makes the bedroom more harmonious, and the bed is now a comforting and private cocoon for reading, playing, and sleeping. With curtains that open and close like those in a puppet theater, the bed offers endless opportunities for children's creative fun.

SUPPLIES

From IKEA:
- *Kura* reversible bed
- *Hugad* curtain rod (80 in./200 cm)
- Two 40 x about 32-in./100 x about 80-cm curtains

Other:
- Wallpaper that matches the bedroom walls
- Wallpaper paste
- Paint
- Screws

TOOLS:
- Utility knife (for the wallpaper)
- Paste brush
- Bucket for the paste
- Paintbrush
- Lightweight rail, if desired
- Pencil
- Ruler
- Awl to mark the placement of the rod
- Screwdriver

CHOOSE ECO-FRIENDLY PRODUCTS WHEN PAINTING YOUR CHILD'S BED.

HOW TO DO IT

1. Before assembling the *Kura* bed, first wallpaper the panels.

2. Paint the structure, following the recommendations of the paint manufacturer, and allow it to dry.

3. Assemble the bed according to the instructions provided.

4. Attach the *Hugad* rod or a lightweight rail on the inside of the bed's topmost horizontal rail.

5. Hang the curtains.

6. Sing a lullaby!

Heute:
Eis
€ 1,50

16-18
Uhr
Happy
Hour

42

Wir
müssen
draussen
bleiben

AS A SAFETY
MEASURE, HIDE ALL
THE LIGHTING'S
ELECTRICAL CABLES
BEHIND PANELING.

The Store

There's a mystery hiding behind designer Oliver Baentsch's cozy playhouse—a secret door concealed by the *Trofast* storage units. Just gently push the left wall, and this nearly invisible door will open, offering up a space for endless hours of playtime. The removable bins can be easily repositioned so that kids can get through!

For more information about this project, go to www.ikeahackers.net/2015/02/diy-playhouse-children.html.

SUPPLIES

From IKEA:

- *Kura* reversible bed
- *Trofast* storage combination (39 x 17³/₈ x 37 in./99 x 44 x 24 cm)
- *Dioder* 4-piece LED light strip set
- *Striberg* LED light strip, aluminum color

Other:

- Plywood paneling or tongue-and-groove boards, ½ in. (13 mm) thick
- 2 x 4-in. (5 x 10-cm) boards for railing and roof framing
- Paint
- Wood glue
- Wood screws
- Magnets for hanging the supermarket sign and attaching the roof shutter
- Suggested decorative elements: Fabric for a curtain (30-in./76-cm square)
- Awning (30 x 50 in./75 x 125 cm), if desired
- Doorbell (optional)

TOOLS:

- Jigsaw
- Miter saw
- Drill
- Clamp
- Level
- Awl
- Tape measure
- Pencil

HOW TO DO IT

1 Assemble the *Kura* bed following the instructions provided.

On the side opposite the ladder, add a vertical 2x4-in. (5x10-cm) board to create a wide opening for access under the bed. Reinforce the structure with a horizontal brace that will also form the bottom sill of the store window.

2 Cut the lumber to create the roof structure using the miter saw. Cut a piece of lumber the width of the bed to make the roof ridge. Glue and screw the lumber to the *Kura* structure and to the roof ridge. Reinforce with one or two horizontal pieces after adjusting their dimensions and ends using the miter saw. Check their position with a level, then glue and screw the connections.

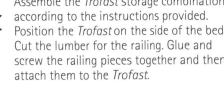

Assemble the *Trofast* storage combination according to the instructions provided. Position the *Trofast* on the side of the bed. Cut the lumber for the railing. Glue and screw the railing pieces together and then attach them to the *Trofast*.

Hang the *Dioder* and *Striberg* light strips to light the space under the bed, installing the electrical equipment on the back wall so children cannot access it. Follow all safety measures. You can also use battery-powered lighting.

Cover the façade and roof with paneling, screwing it to the wood structure. If you'd like, you can create a window on the second floor.

Add your own decorative touches, such as an awning, curtain, and shutters. You could also install a doorbell.

TAKE THE DIY CHALLENGE

KURA

The *Kura* Slide

For this project, Eric Strong drew inspiration from his child's favorite things—playground games, the wire bead maze toy, and secret hiding places—and transformed the *Kura* bed into the ultimate play space for children. Complete with a slide, a door that reveals a secret hideaway, and storage for an endless amount of toys, this project will fulfill children's dreams.

FOR MORE ABOUT THIS INVENTION, WATCH "IKEA HACK—KURA BED WITH SLIDE AND SECRET ROOM" ON YOUTUBE.

SUPPLIES

From IKEA:

• *Trofast* storage combination (39 x 17³/₈ x 37 in./99 x 44 x 94 cm)
• 2 *Kura* reversible beds
• *Bestå* shelf unit
• *Dioder* 4-piece LED light strip set

Other:

• Metal rods (for the secret door hinge and axis, so the crane can pivot)
• Wood paneling
• Sheet of ³/₄-in. (2-cm) -thick plywood (for slide)
• Whiteboard (for slide surface)
• Lumber for the bed guard, the crane, and the frame of the secret doorway
• Boards for the shelves of the secret doorway
• PVC pipes and connectors (for the bead maze)
• Blue adhesive paper
• Light wood stain
• Rope
• Pulley
• Bucket
• Assorted hardware: nails, screws, hinges, latches, anchors
• Wood glue

TOOLS:

• Jigsaw
• Drill
• Pulley block
• Tape measure
• Pencil

HOW TO DO IT

You'll need two *Kura* beds to build this bed with a slide, but you'll only assemble the first one following the manufacturer's instructions—the second bed provides pieces for the rest of the assembly. The other supplies listed are primarily used to build the play elements, including the slide with a pole and pulley, a wire bead maze, and the pivoting door that opens to the secret room located under the bed.

 Assemble the slide: First construct the *Trofast* combination according to the manufacturer's instructions. To build the slide's platform, use the slats from the second *Kura* bed.

 Build the first *Kura* bed according to the manufacturer's instructions, but do not install the bed slats so you can continue to work comfortably in and around the structure. Close up the front using the wood paneling, but leave an opening on the side where the slide will attach. The hole will be hidden behind the *Trofast* bins and will provide a second way out of the secret room. Your child can simply push the bins away and climb out.

 Attach the slide to the assembled loft structure. Cut the whiteboard to the size of the slide and glue it down on top of the plywood.

 Assemble the hinged doorframe for the secret room using the *Bestå* component. Eric hid the latch that opens the door in the pages of a book—a guaranteed surprise for visitors!

 Install the LED lights in the secret room, installing the electrical equipment on the back wall so children cannot access it. Follow all safety measures. You can also use battery-powered lighting.

 Assemble the bed slats in their framework.

Design : Gisela Vidallé

KURA

The Little House

Matte and free of any embellishment, Gisela Vidallé's little house embodies the elegance and simplicity of great masterpieces.

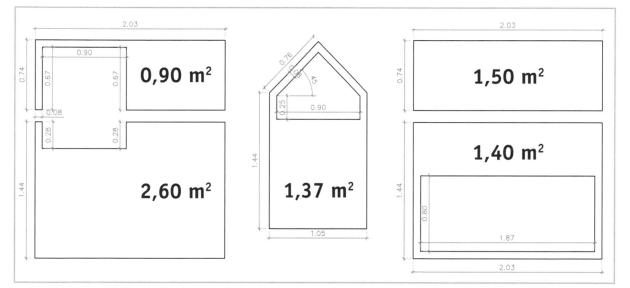

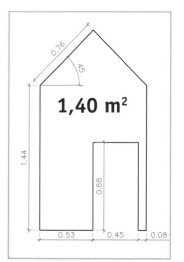

SUPPLIES

From IKEA:
- *Kura* reversible bed

Other:
- 2 x 3-in. (5 x 7.5-cm) lumber for the framework
- Glue
- Wood screws
- Wood filler
- Paint, if desired
- Masking tape
- Medium Density Fiberboard (MDF) panels, ⅜ in. (1 cm) or ½ in. (13 mm) thick
- Finish of your choice
- 12-volt LED light strips

TOOLS:
- Jigsaw
- Circular saw
- Drill
- Awl to mark the placement of the screws
- Tape measure
- Paintbrush and painting supplies, if desired
- Miter saw, if desired

HOW TO DO IT

THE *KURA* BED IS ALMOST COMPLETELY HIDDEN INSIDE THE WOOD SHELL.

Assemble the *Kura* bed using the instructions provided. Add glue and screws for reinforcement.

Use lumber to make the roof structure, and attach it to the bed. See the diagrams on pages 173 and 175 for dimensions. Glue and screw all connections.

Countersink the pilot holes and cover the screw heads with wood filler. If you wish, you can paint the whole structure.

Measure the outside dimensions of each of the four sides of the bed and the sloping sides of the roof. Cut the MDF panels to size, and cut out the doors, the windows, and the ladder as shown in the diagrams on pages 173 and 175. For a cleaner look, miter the panel edges.

Glue and screw the paneling to the frame.

Apply the finish of your choice.

Complete the project by installing LED light strips to light the space under the bed. Follow all safety measures.

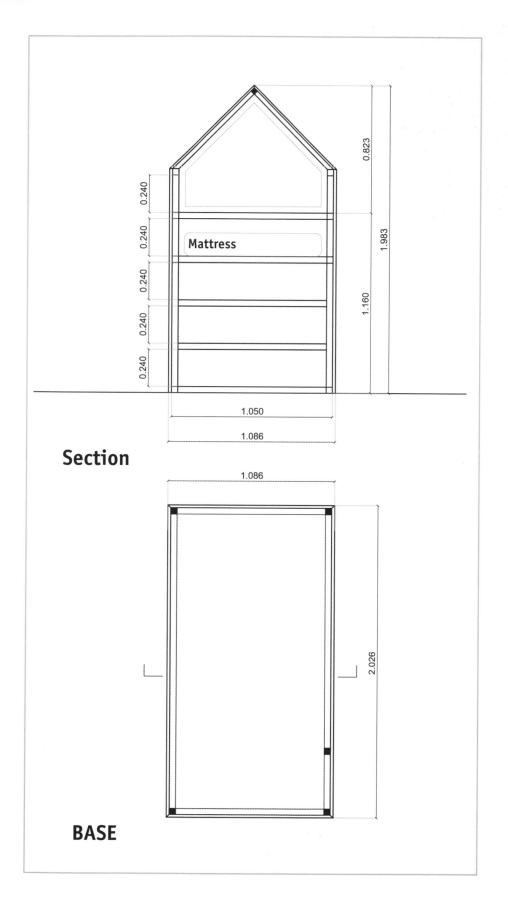

0.823

0.240

0.240

Mattress

0.240

0.240

0.240

1.983

1.160

1.050

1.086

Section

1.086

2.026

BASE

level

EXPERT

THE DOUBLE-DECKER CABIN

© Inter IKEA Systems B.V.

Who doesn't dream about sleeping in a cabin, with open windows letting in fresh air and the sounds of nature lulling you to sleep? This project lets you bring that atmosphere into your home in the form of a bunk bed. Although it is cost-effective and easy to tackle, this bed does require some time and attention during construction. Make sure everything is properly secured, because a cabin is also meant for playing!

HOW TO DO IT

HERE'S A REAL CABIN FOR CHILDREN TO CAMP INDOORS.

1 Assemble the bunk bed frame according to the manufacturer's instructions. Prepare the pre-cut plywood components according to the dimensions illustrated below. If you wish, you can paint them now, or you can wait until after the building is complete.

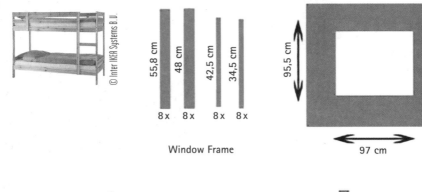

© Inter IKEA Systems B.U.

55,8 cm — 8x
48 cm — 8x
42,5 cm — 8x
34,5 cm — 8x

Window Frame

95,5 cm
97 cm
2x

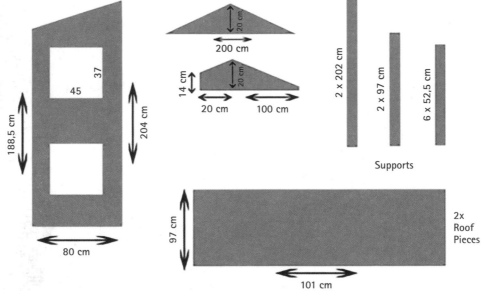

188,5 cm
80 cm
204 cm
45
37

200 cm
20 cm
14 cm
20 cm
20 cm
20 cm
100 cm

2 x 202 cm
2 x 97 cm
6 x 52,5 cm

Supports

97 cm
101 cm
2x Roof Pieces

2 Make the roof structure: Place four vertical wood supports on the bedposts using mounting plates or dowel connections.

Attach a vertical support to the back of the bed to support the horizontal panel.

Attach the triangles on top.

Adjust the roof on the framework using brackets or metal corners.

Attach the vertical boards with the windows on the side of the bed and to the left in front. Decorate with slats of different widths (beveled edges will be prettier).

If you didn't paint before assembling the cabin, apply a coat of primer and a coat of paint, and allow to dry.

Install the curtain rods and hang the curtains.

SUPPLIES

From IKEA:
- *Mydal* bunk bed frame

Other:
- Pre-cut ½-in. (13-mm) plywood. Refer to drawing opposite for quantities and dimensions.
- 1 x 4-in. (2.5 x 10-cm) lumber for the supports and window frames
- Mounting plates (or dowels and wood glue)
- Screws
- Brackets or metal corners
- Medium and fine sandpaper
- 2 slats for decorating windows (refer to orange drawing for quantities and dimensions)
- Primer and paint
- Curtain rods
- Curtains

TOOLS:
- Jigsaw (if you're cutting the wood yourself)
- Screwdriver
- Drill
- Tape measure
- Pencil
- Clamps
- Paintbrush or roller

FACE-TO-FACE DRAFTING TABLES

Photos : © Inter IKEA Systems B.U.

This drafting table designed by architect Erik Johnson is proof that you can make complex furniture using commonplace supplies and only a few pieces of wood. Like carpentry inventions of the past, which were dictated more by ingenuity than technology, you can raise and lower the tabletops and modify the angle of both of the work surfaces.

Design : Erik Johnson

© Photos : Stonetentarchitecture.com

HOW TO DO IT

 Build a rectangular frame with a lateral brace for reinforcement using the 2x3 lumber.

Install the center shelf for drawing supplies

 Attach a triangular piece of wood to each corner of the frame, then attach the table legs to the triangles.

 Attach two side pieces to the center shelf to keep supplies from falling off.

 THE TABLETOP AND ITS MECHANISM

Cut each tabletop to 19½ in. (49.5 cm) wide. Attach the hinges to the tabletops, then to the frame (ask another person to help hold the tabletop in the correct position).

 Cut the lumber for the height adjustment levers and screw three coat hooks to each. Attach the levers to the tabletops using a hinge.

 Screw in the carriage bolts into the side of the frame. They will be used to hold the levers when changing the angle of the tabletop. Install one lever first. Make sure it's in the proper position and that it works before installing the second one in the same manner.

ATTACH A RAIL TO THE BOTTOM OF THE TABLETOP TO KEEP PENCILS FROM ROLLING OFF.

SUPPLIES

From IKEA:
- 2 *Gerton* tabletops
- 4 *Sjunne* legs
- 2 *Ingolf* junior chairs
- *Ordning* kitchen utensil holders

Other:
- 2 x 3-in. (2 x 7.5-cm) softwood or laminated lumber, for the frame
  - 2 pieces cut to 37½ in. (95 cm)
  - 2 pieces cut to 53 in. (135 cm)
  - 1 piece cut to 35 in. (89 cm), for the reinforcement brace
- 1 piece ¾ x 5½-in. (2 x 14-cm) softwood or laminated lumber cut to 53 in. (135 cm), for the shelf
- ¾ x 1½-in. (2 x 4-cm) softwood or laminated lumber
  - 2 pieces cut to about 53 in. (135 cm), for the sides of the shelf (actual length must be based on the placement of the frame's lateral supports)
  - 4 pieces cut to about 24 in. (61 cm), for the adjustment levers (actual length must be based on the largest angle desired for the tabletop incline)
- ¾ x 2½-in. (2 x 6.5-cm) softwood or laminated lumber, for the braces (length of the braces must be based on the actual measurements between the table legs)
  - 2 pieces cut to about 36 in. (91.5 cm), for the corner braces
  - 1 piece cut to about 51½ in. (131 cm), for the central brace connecting the corner braces
- 5 wide hinges (tabletop)
- 4 narrow hinges (levers)
- 12 coat hooks
- 4 carriage bolts with washers and nuts
- Screws

TOOLS:
- Table saw or circular saw to cut the tabletops
- Circular saw or jigsaw to cut the lumber
- Drill
- Tape measure

A BOWL LAMP!

© Inter IKEA Systems B.V.

> The standing lamp in all its breadth and majesty reigns over many a living room. Determined to avoid cliché, Tim Castelijn dove into an entirely personal interpretation of the light. Made from wood and topped with a salad bowl, it's both a prototype and an archetype.

AN ADJUSTABLE
LAMP THAT RIVALS
THE GREAT DESIGNS
OF HOME DÉCOR.

Design : Tim Castelijn

© Photos : Tim Castelijn / www.timcastelijn.nl

HOW TO DO IT

Base

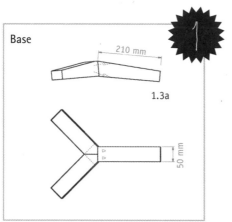

210 mm

1.3a

50 mm

BASE

1. Cut two 8¼-in. (21-cm) pieces of wood from the block and bevel one end of each at a 45-degree angle.

2. Cut a third 8-in. (20-cm) piece from the block, and bevel one end at a 5-degree angle.

3. Using a plane, thin the top of all three elements, keeping in mind that the third piece cannot be less than about 1½ in. (4 cm) high in order for it to support the lamp column.

4. Attach the wide ends of the two 45-degree bevels, using glue and at least two anchors, to form a V.

5. Cut the point of the V where it measures 2 in. (5 cm) in width.

6. Screw the third element to the point of the V so the three elements slope gently downward.

COLUMN

1. In two pieces of 35½-in. (90-cm) -long lumber, drill a ⅜-in. (1-cm) hole 2 in. (5 cm) from the upper ends. Make sure the holes are perfectly aligned. The arm won't articulate if they are not. A drill press is helpful for this step.

2. On a 7½-in. (19-cm) piece of lumber, draw transversal lines at the following intervals: ¾ in. (2 cm), 2⅜ in. (6 cm), 4¾ in. (12 cm) and 6¾ in. (17 cm). Cut triangles into the wood so a row of regular notches results.

3. Place this piece 19 in. (48 cm) from the base between the two other pieces you prepared to form the column. Make sure that the two column pieces are perfectly aligned before attaching them with glue and screws.

4. Insert the third element of the base between the posts of the column, and attach them using four screws per side.

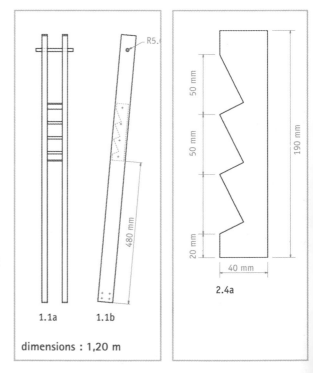

R5.

50 mm

50 mm

20 mm

480 mm

190 mm

40 mm

2.4a

1.1a   1.1b

dimensions : 1,20 m

ARM

1. Take two 31½-in. (80-cm) pieces of lumber. On one, make a mark at about 5 in. (13 cm) from one end where you will place the second piece of lumber.

2. Measure and mark 27½ in. (70 cm) on the column pieces. Use a plane to reduce the thickness of a 2 x 2 x 4 in. (5 x 5 x 10 cm) block of wood at an angle of 4 or 5 degrees. Insert the block between the posts of the column and stop reducing the block when it fits snugly between the posts.

3. Attach the two pieces of lumber you prepared for the arm to the block using glue and screws.

4. Drill a ³⁄₈-in. (1-cm) hole through the block. Align the holes in the column with the hole in the block and attach the arm.

5. Attach the metal support arm.

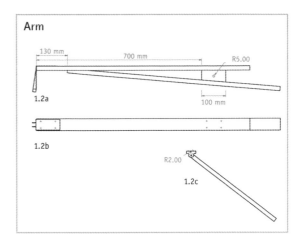

Arm

130 mm · 700 mm · R5.00

1.2a · 100 mm

1.2b

R2.00 · 1.2c

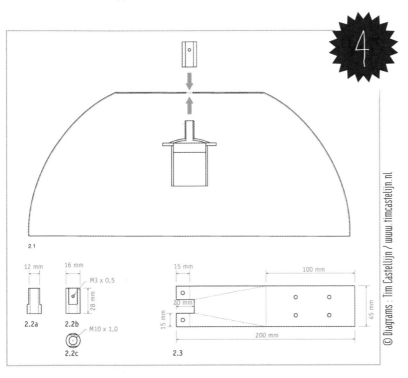

2.1

12 mm · 16 mm · M3 x 0,5 · 28 mm

2.2a · 2.2b · M10 x 1,0

2.2c

15 mm · 100 mm

20 mm · 45 mm

15 mm · 200 mm

2.3

© Diagrams : Tim Castelijn / www.timcastelijn.nl

SHADE AND HINGE

1. Drill a ³⁄₈-in. (1-cm) hole in the middle of the salad bowl.

2. Secure the *Hemma* bulb socket on the inside of the salad bowl and attach the power cord to the socket. (If you are not comfortable with basic wiring techniques, consult an electrician.)

3. Use a folded metal plate as shown in the drawing (or hardware of your choice) to attach the socket assembly to the arm of the lamp.

For more information about this project, go to timcastelijn.nl.

SUPPLIES

From IKEA:
- *Blanda Blank* salad bowl
- *Hemma* cord set
- *Ledare* LED lightbulb

Other:
- 26 x 3 x 3-in. (66 x 7.6 x 7.6-cm) softwood block, for the base
- Wood glue
- Wood anchors
- Screws
- Four pieces of ¾ x 2 x 35¼-in. (1.8 x 5 x 90-cm) softwood lumber
- 2 x 2 x 4-in. (5 x 5 x 10-cm) softwood block, for the arm
- Metal support arm
- Bolts
- 12–18 ft. of electrical wire
- Switch
- Plug
- ¾ x 1¾-in. (2 x 4.5-cm) metal plate

TOOLS:
- Small wood saw
- Tape measure
- Pencil
- Drill
- Drill press
- Plane
- Screwdriver
- Metal saw
- Wire cutter

THE ARTAV BOOKSHELF

© Inter IKEA Systems B.V.

© Photos et dessins : Atelier 4/5

Création : Atelier 4/5

❝❞ An anagram is an act of transgression. Combining coincidence and mathematical probability, the rules of an anagram dictate that nothing be added or removed from the starting element. It's just about composing it differently. That's the challenge the designers at Atelier 4/5 took on when they transformed the *Tarva* five-drawer dresser into the Artav bookshelf. It's an anagram—but also a piece of furniture.

HOW TO DO IT

Throw the dresser assembly instructions in the trash! Before assembling, paint the components and prepare the wood. For each step that follows, glue, screw, and secure each element with clamps for the amount of time recommended by the wood glue manufacturer.

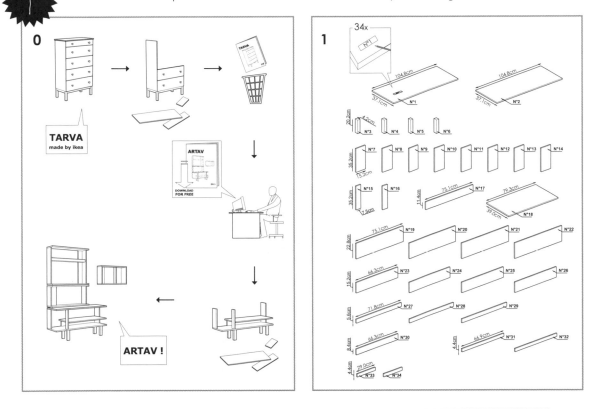

SUPPLIES

From IKEA:
- *Tarva* 5-drawer chest (31¹⁄₈ x 50 x 15³⁄₈ in./ 79 x 127 x 39 cm)

Other:
- Paint
- Masking tape

- Wood glue
- Wood screws

TOOLS:
- Paintbrush or small roller
- Drill
- Clamps
- Awl
- Tape measure
- Pencil

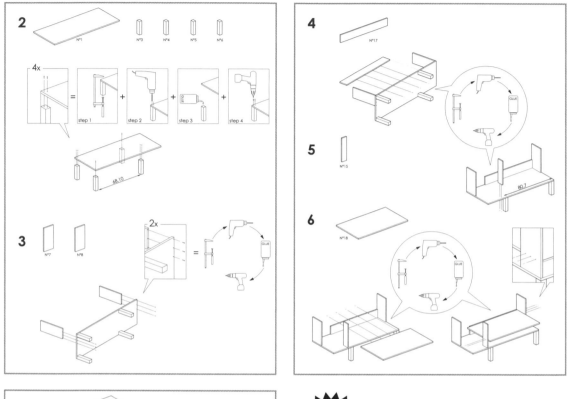

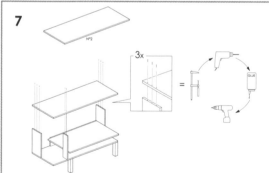

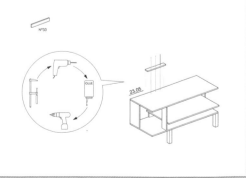

Start with the base component: Glue the four feet onto the dresser's side panel (Image 2).

The sides of the drawers become the sides of the shelves (Image 3).

Reinforce the support with a batten placed at two-thirds the length of the shelves (Images 4–5).

Continue to add the pieces as shown in the diagrams to finish the bottom component (Images 6–9).

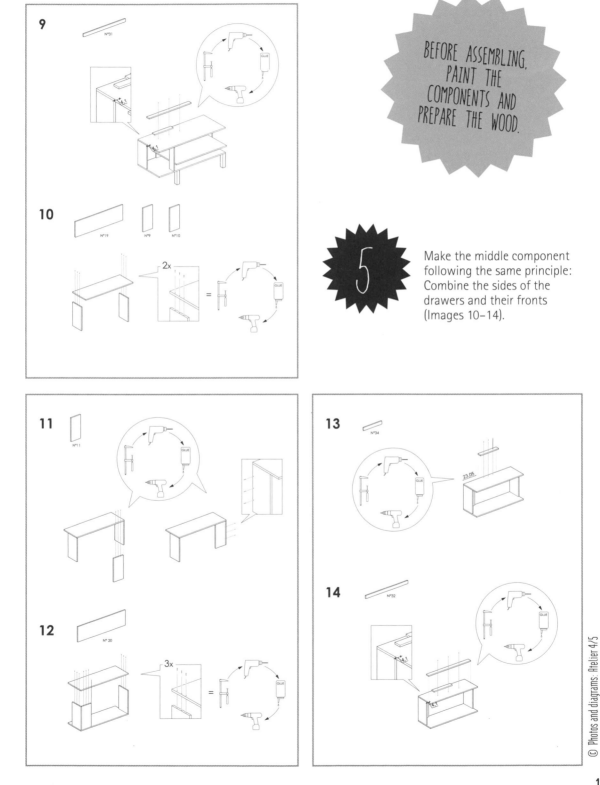

BEFORE ASSEMBLING,
PAINT THE
COMPONENTS AND
PREPARE THE WOOD.

Make the middle component following the same principle: Combine the sides of the drawers and their fronts (Images 10–14).

193

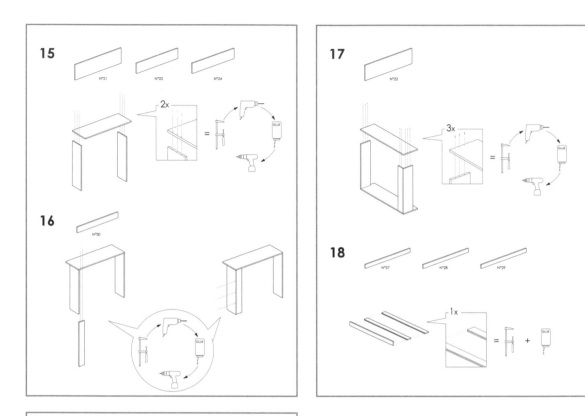

Make the upper component in the same way, this time using two of the drawer's backs as the sides of the shelves (Images 14–18).

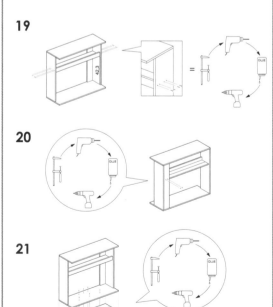

Make the middle shelf for the upper component. Attach at two-thirds the height of the component (Images 18–20).

You can download a larger copy of these plans at http://atelier4cinquieme.be/sites/atelier4cinquieme.be/files/pdf/atelier4cinquieme_artav_ikea_design_mobilier_0.pdf.

22

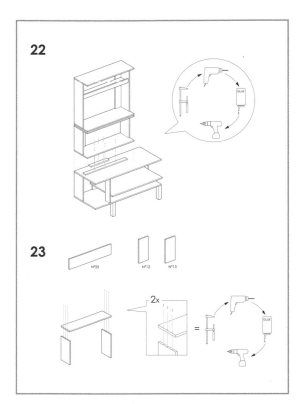

23

Attach the upper component to the middle component using two supports: one short, one long (Images 21–22).

Attach the middle element to the base, repeating the same procedure (Image 22).

You can make an extra shelf with the remaining pieces (Images 23-25).

24

25

BONUS

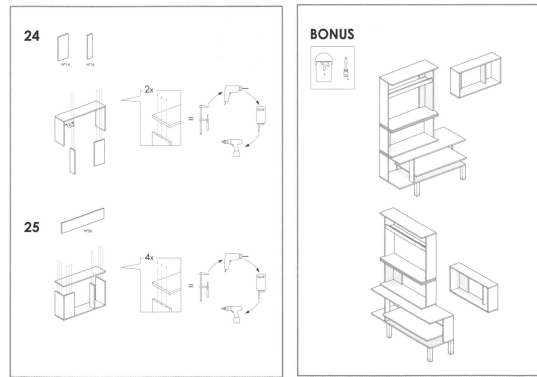

"MARK MY WORDS"
CHAIR

© Inter IKEA Systems B.U.

" Like Marcel Duchamp's bottle rack, many common pieces of furniture have had uncommon careers. Will IKEA's readily available pencils come into such fame? Their small size makes them seem disposable: you use one, then you toss it. Or maybe you slip it into your pocket like artist Florian Alexander Fuchs did. Florian gathered more than 6,971 pencils from IKEA—but all in the name of art. In 2013, Florian designed a chair made from these pencils. Known as *Størenfried*, or "troublemaker," the chair took more than four weeks to complete, and you could say it's more pointed than subversive art.

TAKE THE DIY CHALLENGE

Design : Florian Alexander Fuchs

© Photos : http://www.florian-alexander-fuchs.com

FLORIAN ALEXANDER FUCH'S CHAIR WAS A TOP-TEN HONOREE IN IKEA'S 2013 SPACE FOR IDEAS DESIGN COMPETITION, ORGANIZED BY THE IKEA FOUNDATION IN GERMANY.

HOW TO DO IT

THE CHAIR FRAME:

Decide on the dimensions for your chair. Florian's design is 29³/₈ in. (73.5 cm) wide, 36¼ in. (96 cm) deep, and 30 in. (75 cm) high.

1. Cut the bars using a metal-cutting circular saw, then solder or weld them together to form the frame.

2. Size the frame so the pencils will stick out slightly from the edge of the seat. This will lend lightness to the completed piece.

3. Paint the frame.

THE POLYSTYRENE FORM:

4. Draw the form of the seat on a sheet of polystyrene, then cut out the shape with a box cutter or saw. This step requires several test runs at full size. Use the most comfortable and ergonomic form for your final design.

5. Reproduce the selected form on several sheets of polystyrene, then glue them together to create a stencil.

THE COLLAGE OF PENCILS:

6. Flip over the polystyrene form and attach the first layer of pencils using fence staples (U-shaped nails). Glue the second layer by overlapping the pencils such that you can remove the fence staples from the first layer after the glue is dry. Each pencil should be individually glued in two places.

7. Repeat until you have seven layers of pencils. Once the seventh layer has dried, position the chair frame and attach using construction adhesive or epoxy.

8. Glue seven additional layers of pencils on top of the frame, following the same method as before, securing the frame between the pencil layers.

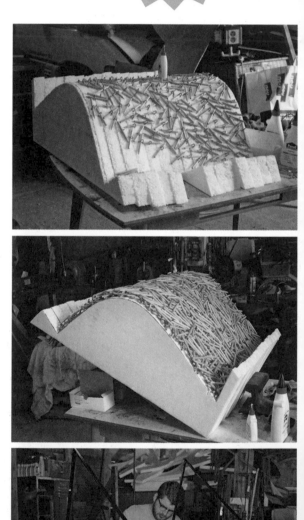

THE FINAL TOUCHES:

9. Turn the chair back onto its feet. Cut the polystyrene sheets one by one and remove the pieces from the chair. Brush clean.

Note: To make the chair as sturdy as possible, Florian glued each individual pencil in two places. He also positioned each pencil one at a time to ensure maximum contact with the layer underneath. If you follow this technique, the chair will be very strong.

SUPPLIES

From IKEA:
• 6,971 IKEA pencils (not one less!)

Other:
• 80 in. (2 m) of steel hexagonal bar
• Paint for metal
• Sheets of polystyrene to make the chair (enough to allow for multiple versions)

• Construction adhesive or quick-set epoxy
• Fence staples (U-shaped nails)
• 7 quarts (6.6 L) of wood glue

TOOLS:
• Metal-cutting circular saw
• Soldering or welding equipment
• Box cutter or saw, for cutting the polystyrene form

A WELL-BALANCED KITCHEN

TAKE THE
DIY
CHALLENGE

Design : Francesco Pepa

❝ The designer Francesco Pepa's elegant kitchen is as light as the designer's free spirit. With its play on configuration and balance, this is almost more of a work of art than a kitchen. It's equipped with all the basic elements: exposed shelving, storage bins, a sink, a stovetop, and even planters for fresh herbs. With its functionality, adaptability, and modern, compact appearance, this kitchen fits nicely in urban homes that are tight on space.

HOW TO DO IT

Drill the legs of the *Norden* table to install the *Ersätta* candleholders (or four solid metal feet, if you prefer). This raises the table and adjusts it to a more comfortable height.

To install the sink and cooktop, cut openings in the tabletop following the provided instructions. Use any templates supplied by the manufacturer.

Prepare the wood (stain and/or varnish) if you wish.

Assemble the remaining IKEA objects according to the manufacturer's instructions. Once assembled, securely screw them to the table. Cut the columns of the *Hektar* floor lamps at two different heights. Be careful not to damage the lamp wiring while cutting the columns.

To connect the sink and cooktop, use a licensed plumber and electrician.

THIS TRANSPORTABLE KITCHEN HIGHLIGHTS THE FUNCTION OF EACH INDIVIDUAL ELEMENT, AND IT CAN BE ADJUSTED TO SUIT YOUR NEEDS (AND WANTS) IN THE KITCHEN.

© Photos : Teste di Legno

SUPPLIES

From IKEA:

- *Norden* extendable table
- 4 *Ersätta* block candleholders
- *Domsjö* sink bowl
- *Nutid* 4-element induction cooktop
- *Glittran* kitchen faucet
- 2 *Hektar* floor lamps
- *Socker* watering can

- *Hyllis* shelving unit
- *Trofast* storage combination with pine finish and boxes
- *Fintorp* rail
- *Stolmen* hook for hanging the watering can
- *Socker* flower box with holder

Other:

- Lumber
- Stain or varnish, if desired
- Wood screws and anchors

Alternative: Instead of candleholders, table feet that can more easily bear the weight of the unit.

TOOLS:

- Drill
- Jigsaw
- Awl
- Screwdriver
- Tape measure
- Pencil

THE PATCHWORK CABINET

LE FIGARO

Design : Francesco Pepa

This unusual cabinet was assembled from small storage units joined to one another with screws, bolts, and nuts. The assortment presents storage options for endless types of objects and can easily be labeled as "multifunctional." This might not be the most practical cabinet, but it is the most eccentric. If you're inspired, go ahead and design your own patchwork cabinet. The designer combined a nightstand, lamp, filing cabinet, and more to create this piece, but don't be limited by what you see.

HOW TO DO IT

1. Enlist the help of a partner to assemble this unit, specifically to hold the units in place while you screw them down. Do not attempt to build it on your own!

2. Start at the bottom, using three *Ekby Valter* brackets as feet. For the fourth foot, the designer used an unusual object—a mustard jar. Remember to empty it before installing! Add an *Ekby* behind the mustard jar for reinforcement.

3. Build each storage element according to the instructions provided. Saw feet or other supports to attach to lower elements and secure in place. Cut a circle through the top of the nightstand for the lamp.

4. Attach the napkin holders to create a newspaper and letter rack. Assemble the table following the manufacturer's instructions.

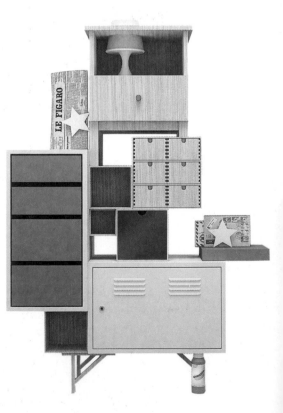

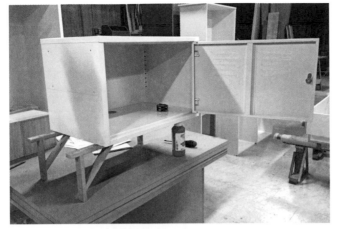

A FLUID CREATION THAT FLAUNTS YOUR SENSE OF HUMOR.

SUPPLIES

From IKEA:

- 4 *Ekby Valter* brackets (7 in./18 cm high)
- *Senap Mild* mustard container
- *Tarva* nightstand
- *Lampan* table lamp
- 2 *Fantastisk* napkin holders (or a style similar to what's pictured)
- *IKEA PS* metal cabinet
- *Lack* wall shelf
- *Micke* drawer unit on casters

Other:

- 3 wood rack units, CD format
- Mini chest of drawers (similar in style to the *Moppe* mini chest of drawers, which is not available in the US)
- Screws
- Bolts
- Nuts

TOOLS:

- Jigsaw
- Awl
- Screwdriver
- Tape measure
- Pencil
- Compass
- Glue
- Clamps

CONVERTIBLE SITTING-STANDING DESK

TAKE THE
DIY
CHALLENGE

Design : Kelli Anderson

As a modern person, you have but one loyal friend—your desk. You spend most of your time at it, soak it with coffee, and entrust it with your dreams and strategies. This essential part of daily life has but one fault: You have to stay seated, which inevitably brings the physical discomfort of back pain. But if reducing the time you spend at your desk is out of the question, how can you lessen the impact all this sitting has on your health? Just make your desk adjustable, using a jack to change its height. The standing position will improve your metabolism and promote concentration, but you'll still have the option to sit. This take on the convertible desk by Kelli Anderson deserves a standing ovation.

HOW TO DO IT

Kelli Anderson hired a carpenter to make her sit-stand desk, and unless you're a pro, we highly encourage you to do the same. However, anyone can construct the interior compartments and tabletop.

First, draw plans using software, like Google SketchUp, to determine what you need to buy. Kelli chose to put her computer on a height-adjustable component. Then she positioned IKEA kitchen cabinets complete with drawers on either side of the adjustable element. To construct the unit, first attach the rails to the wall, followed by the furniture. Install the countertop and lateral panels last.

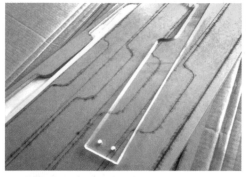

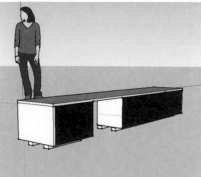

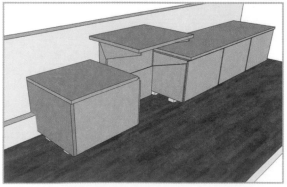

COMBINE AND ADAPT THE KITCHEN UNITS AND ACCESSORIES TO MEET YOUR DESK NEEDS.

SUPPLIES

From IKEA:

FOR THE COMPARTMENTS AND DESKTOP:

• 4 *Sektion* base cabinets with 2 doors (width: 31½ in./80 cm; depth 23½ in./60 cm; height 23½ in./60 cm)
• *Sektion* drawers and accessories (The drawer dimensions depend on the slide tracks you choose. Full extension tracks will better suit large drawers.)
• *Saljan* kitchen countertop (custom cut)

Other:

• Pre-cut lateral panels

FOR THE DRAWERS:

• Slide tracks and supplies
• Transparent glue for plastic materials
• Clear acrylic sheets for the drawer bottoms
• Sides with pre-cut grooves
• Handles

ASSEMBLING A DRAWER:

Slide the bottom into the side grooves, then attach the side and bottom.

ANOTHER SOLUTION:

Rather than building your own drawers, use a piece of furniture with drawers and insert it into your component.

For information about how Kelli and her carpenter built the height-adjustable component, see http://kellianderson.com/blog/2013/12/a-stand-up-desk-ikea-hack.

LIST OF PROJECTS

CREDITS

Pages 6, **7**, **8**, **10**, **12**, **14**, **16**, **18**, **20**, **22**, **24 g.**, **25 g.**, **26**, **28 h.**, **30**, **32 g.**, **33 g.**, **34**, **36**, **38**, **41**, **50**, **51**, **52**, **56**, **58**, **60**, **62 g.**, **64**, **66**, **68**, **70**, **72**, **74**, **76**, **80**, **82**, **84**, **86**, **88**, **90 g.**, **92**, **94**, **97**, **116**, **117**, **118**, **122**, **124**, **126**, **128**, **132**, **136**, **140**, **144**, **148**, **152**, **156**, **158**, **161**, **176**, **177**, **178**, **182**, **186**, **190 g.**, **196**, **200**, **204**, **208** © Inter IKEA Systems B.V. **3** "Adjustable Lamp" © Tim Castelijn - www.timcastelijn.nl / **9** "Black Stickers on a White Malm Drawer" © 2015 photo Maria Rosenlöf - www.mariarosenlof.com © 2015 Therese Larsson - www.theresel.se / **11** "The Wooden Cutlery" © Photo IKEA Livet Hemma © Inter IKEA Systems B.V 2014 / **13** "Alseda Toys Storage" © Rosandra Ferri - mommodesign.com / **15** "The Cutting Boards" © Photo IKEA Livet Hemma © Inter IKEA Systems B.V 2013 / **17** "Train Storage" © Abby Lawson - www.justagirlandherblog.com / **19** "Micke Desk, Mondrian" IKEA Livet Hemma Blog © Photo Nina Broberg © Inter IKEA Systems B.V 2013 / **21** "Skapa" © Sam Johnson - www.samjohnsondesign.com / **23** "Sharpie Chair" © Caitlin Wilson / **24 d.** "Rabbit Fado" © Rosandra Ferri - mommodesign.com / **25 d.** "Moon Fado" © Rosandra Ferri - mommodesign.com © Martin Krusche / **27** "Plates Wall Decoration" IKEA Livet Hemma Blog © Photo Nina Broberg © Inter IKEA Systems B.V 2012 / **31** "Painted Crockery" © Nadia Soledad Anton - www.megustaonomegusta.com.ar / **32 d.** "Drommar Light Garland" © Rosandra Ferri - mommodesign.com / **33 d.** "Heart Lamp" © Rosandra Ferri - mommodesign.com / **35** "Jokkmokk Table Ikea Hack" © Regina Morrison - Acute Designs - www.acutedesigns.org / **37** "Ikea Hack - Cake Plate" © Masni Dekoráció / **39** "Bureau enfant" © Cynthia Idels Hamelle for *Peek It Magazine* / **42**, **43**, **44**, **45** "Rekordit" © Shane Keaney - SK - ShaneKeaney.com / **46** "Meuble Vintage By Daily Slices" © Anna Pasco - Blog Daily Slices - www.daily-slices.fr / **48** "Compact cabinet with Kallax" © Agnes Hammar - hejregina. elledecoration.se / **53**, **54**, **55** "Knuff Transformable Coffee Table" © Kenneth Yeoh (Malaysia) / **57** "Paper Lamp" © Marianne Norup - www.dig-mig.no / **59** "Pax goes Baroque" © Ewa Pettersson - menoform.com / **61** "Suspender Curtains" © Photo Heather Weston © Amanda Kingloff - projectkid.com / **62 d.**, **63** "Lillabo Train Set" © Rosandra Ferri - mommodesign.com / **65** "Jouets détournés. Faîtes vos jeux p.063" © Marie Claire copyright.com - Pellerin J.B. - Loiseau A. - Turbé D. / **67** "Boîte lumineuse" © Anne-Sophie Michat and Carine Keyvan - Hëllø Blogzine / **69** "Bekväm Stool" © Rosandra Ferri - mommodesign.com / **71** "Toolbench for Kids" © Cecilia Thorsell - Fruthorsell.wordpress.com / **73** "Multi Color Ivar dressers" IKEA Livet Hemma Blog © Photo Nina Broberg ©Inter IKEA Systems B.V 2011 / **75** "House Cabins" © Marie Willumsen / **77**, **78**, **79** "Faux Marble Docksta Table" © Danika Herrick - danikaherrick.com / **81** "Jellyfish Light" © Brenna Berger Design - brennabergerdesign.com / **83** "Bookshelf - Una Libreria" © Francesco Pepa - Teste Di Legno / **85** "Kids Play Kitchen" © Anna Krigh - Haga 26 / **87** "Horloge suspendue" © Hélène Grimaud and Julien Schwartzmann - Création www.heju.fr / **89** "The Customized Lack Tables" © Photo IKEA Livet Hemma © Inter IKEA Systems B.V 2013 / **90 d.**, **91** "Transforming Maskros Pendant Lamp - Maskros XL" © normal arhitektura - www.normal.ba / **93** "Workspace for LEGO Creators" © Martin Storbeck - http://retiredbricks. com / **95** "Fruit welcome mats" © Création originale Brittany Watson Jepsen - thehousethatlarsbuilt.com © Photos Julia Lamotte / **98**, **99**, **100**, **101** "Wandregal - Frosta X" © Andreas Bhend - www. andreasbhend.ch / **102**, **103**, **104**, **105** "Luge" © Le Fab Shop - Samuel Bernier & Andreas Bhend (www.andreasbhend.ch) / **106**, **107**, **108**, **109**, **110**, **111** "Draisienne" © Le Fab Shop - Samuel Bernier & Andreas Bhend / **112**, **113** "Children's Desk" © Maria Cañal Garcia - escarabajosbichosymariposas.com / **114**, **115** "Frosta Swing" © Rosandra Ferri - mommodesign.com / **119**, **120**, **121** "Reclaimed Wood Buffet" © Aniko Levai - Place of my Taste/ **123** © Photo Anna Kern © Styling Benedikte Ugland and Linda Åhman / **125** "The Rast Chest of Drawers in Fake Wood" © Photo IKEA Livet Hemma © Inter IKEA Systems B.V 2011 / **127** "Un Godmorgon chic et boisé" © Annie Cournoyer - voixdeplume.com / **129**, **130**, **131** "Big Lampan Lamps" © Daniel P. Saakes / **133**, **134**, **135** "Farmhouse Table" © Monica Mangin - East Coast Creative / **137**, **138**, **139** "Trofast Studio" © Rosandra Ferri - mommodesign.com / **141**, **142**, **143** "Dear Max Light" © Uber Design House - uberdesignhouse.org / **145**, **146**, **147** "DIY IKEA Sewing Table" © Marta Strzeszewski - www.frommartawithlove.com (Denver, Colorado) / **149**, **150**, **151** "Hyllis Ikea Hack" © Soffia Gardarsdottir - www. skreytumhus.is / **153**, **154**, **155** "Kitchen Island" © Danny Cerezo - CS Design - www.candsdesign.com / **157**, **159** "Flat Packed Rearranged - The Ikea Project" © Studio Kieren Jones / **162** "Kura Bed Hack" © Emma Silver - http://frusilver.se / **164**, **165**, **166**, **167** "DIY Playhouse for Kids" © Oliver Baentsch / **168**, **170**, **171** "Kura Hideaway and Play Structure" © Eric Strong / **172**, **173**, **175** "Little Forest House" © Gisela Vidallé - Llonch + Vidallé Architecture - www.llonch-vidalle.com / **179**, **180**, **181** "Bunkbed" © Photo www.kiyomiyui.com © Design Myrthe Smit - www.studiosoet.nl / **183**, **184**, **185** "Multi-Kid Drafting Table" © Erik Johnson - Stone Tent Architecture - stonetentarchitecture.com / **187**, **188**, **189** "Adjustable Lamp" © Tim Castelijn - www.timcastelijn.nl / **190 d.**, **191**, **192**, **193**, **194**, **195** "'TARVA' goes 'ARTAV'" © Atelier 4/5 / **197**, **198**, **199** "Størenfried IKEA Pencil Chair" © Florian Alexander Fuchs - http://www.florian-alexander-fuchs.com / **201**, **202**, **203**, **205**, **206**, **207** "Kitchen - Una Cucina" and "Cabinet - Una Credenza" © Francesco Pepa - Teste Di Legno / **209**, **210**, **211** "Standing Desk" © Kelli Anderson